Platform

'A ground-breaking, ambitious and rigorous account of how and why we must take control over contemporary digital technologies.'

—Nick Srnicek, Lecturer in Digital Economy, King's College London and author of *Platform Capitalism*

'A clarion call for hope amid twenty-first-century doom. With analytical flair, he shows that platforms are not invincible and that their infrastructure may be the key to a better world.'

—Phil Jones, author of *Work Without the Worker: Labour in the Age of Platform Capitalism*

'A compelling account of the political struggles that will be needed to challenge capital's control over digital platforms, and an essential read for anyone who believes in technology's emancipatory potential.'

—Wendy Liu, author of *Abolish Silicon Valley: How to Liberate Technology from Capitalism*

'A punchy analysis of the platform economy that offers more than a critique of big tech's vision of our collective future. Muldoon sketches the contours of a democratic socialist alternative.'

—Aaron Benanav, Researcher at Humboldt University of Berlin and author of *Automation and the Future of Work*

'Encourages us to open our minds fully to the possibility of an alternative future, in which technology is put to work for the many, not the few.'

—Lizzie O'Shea, lawyer and author of *Future Histories*

Platform Socialism

How to Reclaim our Digital Future from Big Tech

James Muldoon

PLUTO PRESS

First published 2022 by Pluto Press
New Wing, Somerset House, Strand, London WC2R 1LA

www.plutobooks.com

Material has been reprinted from the following articles and reproduced by kind permission of the publishers: 'Airbnb Has Been Rocked by COVID-19: Do We Really Want to See It Recover?', openDemocracy, 4 April 2020; 'Why We Need Cooperatives for the Digital Economy', Jacobin, 7 May 2020; 'Don't Break Up Facebook – Make It a Public Utility', Jacobin, 16 December 2020.

British Library Cataloguing in Publication Data
A catalogue record for this book is available from the British Library

ISBN   978 0 7453 4695 3   Paperback
ISBN   978 0 7453 4696 0   Hardback
ISBN   978 0 7453 4697 7   EPUB
ISBN   978 0 7453 4698 4   PDF

This book is printed on paper suitable for recycling and made from fully managed and sustained forest sources. Logging, pulping and manufacturing processes are expected to conform to the environmental standards of the country of origin.

Typeset by Stanford DTP Services, Northampton, England

Simultaneously printed in the United Kingdom and United States of America

Contents

Acknowledgements

This book was written during the first lockdown and substantially revised during the second. It benefited from the feedback of three anonymous reviewers from Pluto Press who helped me reshape the central arguments and cut extraneous material. The team at Pluto have been amazingly supportive in seeing the book through the production process.

The argument builds on a line of thought I have been pursuing since 2019 about alternatives to the current organisation of digital platforms. It builds on a theoretical framework I developed in *Building Power to Change the World* and *Council Democracy*. It also draws on commentary I have written for *Open Democracy* and *Jacobin*. Material has been reprinted from the following articles: 'Airbnb Has Been Rocked by COVID-19: Do We Really Want to See It Recover?', *openDemocracy*, 4 April 2020; 'Why We Need Cooperatives for the Digital Economy', *Jacobin*, 7 May 2020; 'Don't Break Up Facebook – Make It a Public Utility', *Jacobin*, 16 December 2020.

The book owes much to the thriving intellectual community at the think tank Autonomy. I am appreciative of those who offered their generous feedback on an early draft of two chapters. Thank you to Will Stronge, Julian Siravo, Stephanie Sherman, Phil Jones, Jack Kellam, Kam Sandhu, Kyle Lewis, Joe Ryle, Lukas Kikuchi, Cosimo Campani, Luiz Garcia, Sonia Balagopalan, Ishan Khurana and all the collaborators and affiliates who have contributed to Autonomy's work over the years.

Phil Jones read and commented on a full draft and made insightful comments that greatly improved the book. Mirjam Müller, Bruno Leipold, Rahel Süss, Roberta Fischli and Steven Klein helped me think through different sections of the book and provided invaluable feedback.

Thank you also to participants in our socialist calculation debate reading group, including Lillian Cicerchia, Tully Rector, Aaron Benanav, Jack Kellam, Natasha Piano, Mirjam and Steven. I have learned a lot from all of your insightful analyses and from reading your work.

I couldn't have asked for a more supportive environment for my teaching and research than with my colleagues at the University of Exeter, Penryn. In particular, Andy Schaap, Clare Saunders and Karen

Scott have offered much advice and support during my first years at the university.

I owe a debt of gratitude to my friends and family for their ongoing support, in particular to my family in Australia who I have not seen since lockdown and miss immensely. To Sarah, Beth, Michael, Stacey, Noah, Catriona and Pete, I promise to give you real birthday presents when I see you and not give you a copy of this book. In London, I have spent much time during lockdown with Lele, Johannes, Marion, Paul, Jeanne, Tom and Nick whose support, kindness and stimulating conversations were a source of inspiration throughout the process.

I also need to acknowledge the important contributions of my two miniature dachshunds, Barcus Aurelius and Karl Barx for their many cuddles and amusing antics. You get away with too much, but you are so damn cute. I take consolation in the fact that I know you didn't choose the naughty boy life, it chose you.

The most important person throughout has been my inspirational wife, Yasamin. Thank you for everything – for all your support, conversations and adventures together. I owe you so much and am so grateful to share my life with you.

Introduction

The most tragic form of loss isn't the loss of security; it's the loss of the capacity to imagine that things could be different.

Ernst Bloch, *The Principle of Hope*

A deep sense of technological determinism pervades our present era. Tech entrepreneurs predict how technology will transform our world for years to come. These silicon prophets concoct grand visions of our automated and bioengineered future with glittery images of luxury and convenience. Technology is habitually cast as an external force developing on its own accord and dragging us along with it. Too often, calls for 'digital transformation' involve us adapting to the demands of new technology rather than us consciously shaping it. In the absence of any bold ideas from politicians, the tech world has claimed ownership over the future tense.

We have come to see it as normal to give up control over our data and allow platform companies to profit from our activity. The exchange appears to be innocent and even beneficial to us – we use a free service and in exchange companies can use information gathered from the platform to sell targeted advertising. We take it for granted that digital platforms should be privately owned fiefdoms ruled by a tech despot, with billions in profits distributed to a few wealthy shareholders. We accept this situation because this is how the technology has always been presented to us. Platform companies established set patterns for how these products would operate at a time when it was still unclear how fundamentally they would transform our lives. As new markets opened up, a generation of entrepreneurs and gurus took advantage of the public's relative ignorance to claim dominance over this new arena of social life.

But we need to confront the threat Big Tech currently poses to our freedom and democracy. While some of the methods are new, we shouldn't allow the technology to obscure the fact that the basic structure is all too familiar. Platform companies set the rules of the game and benefit from the wealth we create. As individual users of the platform we have little power to affect how it is organised. Now we face a dilemma. We have more tools at our disposal but less control over how they are designed. We can communicate with nearly anyone across the globe but can't determine the conditions in which we connect. We use services for free but see little of the value extracted from our digital lives. It has become easier for us to imagine humans living forever in colonies on Mars than exercising meaningful democratic control over digital platforms.

Big Tech promotes ideas of 'global community' and puts forward wholesome images of their companies helping others connect and find belonging in an alienated and globalised world. Despite their litigious campaigns to undermine local governments and evade regulations, tech companies paint themselves as benevolent partners of local communities and facilitators of new forms of tech-enabled social life. By creating the digital infrastructure that facilitates online communities, platform companies have inserted value capture mechanisms between people seeking to interact and exchange online. Digital platforms are tools that enable a more sophisticated business model for exploiting our social interactions and connections with others. Rather than view this as an aberrant form of 'surveillance capitalism' – driven by an alternative logic and responding to fundamentally different imperatives than capitalism itself – it is more accurate to understand this as an extension and intensification of capitalism's central drive of appropriating human life for profit.[1]

Questions of ownership and control have not been at the forefront of debates over technology. Currently, many assume the main problems with big platforms are their privacy breaches, monopolistic practices and surveillance technologies. The answer to these problems is more – and better – regulation by government. But the fact that these are our main concerns reflects a prior victory for Silicon Valley in setting a limited horizon for how we imagine our digital lives. By failing to acknowledge the depth of the crisis, everybody from libertarians like Andrew Yang to social democrats like Elizabeth Warren miss the possibility for more ambitious and effective proposals. We need to shift our focus from 'privacy, data and size' to 'power, ownership and control'. The first set of issues are important, but they're secondary to a deeper set of concerns about who owns the platforms, who has control and who benefits from the status quo. Technology can either be controlled by private companies and used to generate profit for the few, or it can be directed by communities to benefit the many.

Reclaiming our sense of collective self-determination requires a new kind of platform economy. How do we imagine an alternative that is neither private oligarchy nor unaccountable state bureaucracy – an alternative outside of rule by Big Tech or Big State? The answer lies in new forms of participatory and decentralised governance which place human freedom over profits and ensure the benefits of technology are equally distributed. It involves citizens' active participation in the design and control of socio-technical systems rather than their after-the-fact regulation by a technocratic elite. I call this idea *platform socialism* – the organisation of the digital economy through the social ownership of digital assets and democratic control over the infrastructure and systems that govern our digital lives.

Platform socialism describes both an ideal and a process. On the one hand, it functions as a Kantian regulative idea – a goal we strive towards that helps us determine how to engage with immediate challenges. It is an ideal that we may never fully realise, but it stands as a systematic alternative to the status quo. This allows it to be ambitious in its scope but modest and flexible in how it is applied to empirical reality. It provides a bold vision that attempts to unite different forms of localised resistance around a shared vision of a democratic digital future. By serving as a critical tool, it can also expose the limitations of current digital platforms and proposals for reform. It facilitates holistic thinking about the systemic nature of the problems we face and the need for genuine alternatives that fundamentally break with the extractive model of the corporate digital economy. Rather than just trying to fix Facebook, we should start to imagine what better alternatives could take its place.

On the other hand, platform socialism is about reclaiming a long-term counter-hegemonic project for challenging capitalist control over technology. It must be based on political struggles against the concentrated power of capital and efforts to overcome its control over our lives. This movement is not a quest for an ideal or harmonious society but is driven by antagonistic practices and a resistance to commodification and exploitation. It gestures beyond piecemeal reforms and the bland crisis management and troubleshooting that characterises much of our present response to Big Tech. As a process, platform socialism connects the struggles of different policy spheres and addresses these at the level of concrete institutions and practices. It opens up a space of reflection on our vision of the future in order to encourage deliberation and debate. Rather than providing a rigid blueprint, it invites amendments, additions and corrections. Our sketches should be provisional, contestable and part of an ongoing process of discovery and refinement.

The task of engaging in constructive thinking about how to imagine a future socialist society has for a long time been stifled within the movement. Marx and Engels declined to write 'recipes' for the 'cookshops of the future' and concentrated on a detailed analysis of the capitalist economy. They opposed their own scientific socialism to the 'utopian socialism' of those who imagined societies of the future, but who failed to base their theories on the movement of existing social forces. They believed that constructing detailed blueprints required knowledge that we could not have and that new modes of production would emerge naturally from the development of the old ones.

We have good reason to doubt the cogency of what has been called Marx's 'utopophobia'.[2] We should free ourselves from the shackles preventing us from imagining new institutional forms. In addition to offering a negative account of the problematic features of our own society, we should say something positive about what will replace it. The technological determinism of our time increases the urgency for us to imagine different ways in which digital platforms could be organised. There are many existing accounts of what is wrong with Big Tech but few detailed proposals for how these problems should be addressed.

Without a clear vision of the future and an alternative to the ideological framework of 'capitalist realism,' it can be difficult to imagine how another world could be possible.[3] Reflecting on how we want to live can give us a clearer appreciation of what is at stake and make our goals more vivid and tangible. It is strategically unsound to always be on the defensive, waiting to protest the latest round of capitalist tech innovation. We need to challenge the seeming inevitably of technological progress by putting forward our own vision of how tech should be designed and implemented.

It is also essential to bear in mind that the scope of what is considered feasible is itself a contested and ever-shifting political terrain. Images of radical transformation can help shift the Overton window and make space for new demands and ideas for reform. Restricting our sociological imagination to the confines of what the present order would allow leaves us without the resources to imagine the new. Recovering ideas from the past allows us to explore historical roads not taken and cast new light on overlooked possibilities in the present.

Finally, by imagining visions of the future we actively contribute to the task of turning these into reality. By giving us something to strive for they can generate new desires for change and help channel discontent into meaningful action. They open up a space for what philosopher Miguel Abensour called 'the education of our desires' – how utopian thinking can disrupt our taken-for-granted ways of acting and teach us 'to desire better, to desire more, and above all to desire in a different way.'[4]

To this end, platform socialism seeks to achieve six important goals. First, platform socialism is concerned with expanding the realm of human freedom by enabling communities to actively participate in their own self-governance. It is about creating new digital platforms in which citizens can take back control over their services and public spaces. Freedom in this sense must be understood as more than simply the negative liberty of avoiding interference from others.[5] Debates in the digital economy have been oriented around ideas of negative liberty: the right not to be surveilled, to be left alone and to have proprietary rights over our personal data. All of these are important, but this framework neglects more substantive participatory rights to direct and control how platforms operate. A richer conception of freedom includes an idea of actively shaping the major institutions which affect the material conditions of our lives. Before the dominance of a liberal understanding of negative liberty, emancipatory groups strived for a conception of *freedom as collective self-determination*. This idea goes back to the oldest versions of active citizenship in the Athenian polis, but it also resonates with similar conceptions practised by marginalised groups engaged in a struggle for the expansion of their freedom, from workers and women to black freedom activists and decolonisation movements.[6] Freedom in this sense is understood as an ongoing collective struggle and must be practised rather than enjoyed as a passive condition.[7]

Second, it strives for social ownership over digital assets – the critical infrastructure, software and organisations of the digital economy. This is based on the idea that society's wealth is socially produced through everybody's collective and collaborative labour and should therefore be owned in common and used for the benefit of all. Currently, giant platform companies are highly financialised with large market capitalisations and enormous financial power. The socialisation of these digital platforms would expand the autonomy of workers and enable them to benefit from the value of this technology. Social ownership is neither pure state ownership nor worker ownership. Centralising all property in the instrument of the state risks it devolving into a new bureaucracy, whereas pure worker ownership discriminates against the many people who do not engage in full-time paid labour and creates tensions between workers in different parts of the economy. Achieving a degree of diversity of ownership in the platform economy matters because assets range from multi-billion dollar data centres to local on-demand courier services. A broad ecology of social ownership acknowledges the multiple and overlapping associations to which individuals belong and promotes the flourishing of different communities from mutual societies to platform co-operatives, data trusts and international social networks.

Third, platform socialism enacts community control over the governance of digital platforms. Digital platforms should be reformed so they become internally democratic associations that balance the needs of diverse stakeholders including workers, producers, users and local communities. Representing different parties in the democratic governance process is particularly important because digital platforms are designed to bring together a diverse range of people who may have conflicting interests about how the platform operates. Workers should have a large degree of autonomy in how they perform their work, but the operation of the platform needs to be balanced with the interests of different types of users and members of the community. All those whose interests are significantly affected by the operation of a digital platform should have some say in how it operates. How this is realised in practice depends on the size of the community and the nature of the service. Separating questions of ownership and governance is an important step because it enables smaller communities to exercise control over services that may require large amounts of capital investment in digital infrastructure. The move from shareholder primacy over appointing the board of a company to multi-stakeholder governance structures changes the purpose of digital platforms from maximising profit to creating social value.

Fourth, platform socialism seeks to ensure that the social and economic benefits of digital technology are shared more equitably throughout society. In today's platform economy, the value generated by ordinary users of platforms is hoarded by shareholders who benefit from generous payouts and dividends. Socialising these resources would enable the establishment of large digital social wealth funds to provide investment capacity for new infrastructure and projects. Recapturing the wealth produced through the use of technology would allow for new research and development into socially useful services to provide for people's genuine needs. It would also put an end to the exploitation of society's most vulnerable and precarious workers forced into the gig economy. In addition, it puts forward an idea of data not as a commodity but as a collective resource to be held in common and used to empower citizens and help them solve shared problems. A range of associations would exist, some of which would provide benefits to their members while others would seek to generate social value that would benefit all.

Fifth, an emancipatory movement should aim to combat power inequalities based on social hierarchies. The dynamics of capitalist accumulation intersect and reciprocally reinforce other power relations connected to race, gender, sexual orientation and nationality. As a result, the opportunities and benefits of technology are unevenly distributed across the globe. The exploitation experienced by a highly paid software engineer at Google is different from a coder in India, a factory worker in China or a cobalt miner in the Democratic Republic of Congo. Digital platforms have led to the creation of a large global underclass of 'microwork' platform labourers performing monotonous and repetitive tasks for low pay – often women of colour working in precarious conditions.[8] Big Tech is global in scope, but also fundamentally colonial in character.[9] American and Chinese corporations accumulate the vast majority of profits through their ownership of digital infrastructure, software and intellectual property rights, which imposes a condition of permanent dependency on workers in the Global South. Changes in ownership structure do not automatically challenge structures of colonialism, racism and sexism. A commitment to counteracting these power structures needs to be a grounding principle built into the design and implementation of new systems.[10] If not, new platforms may end up reproducing and exacerbating existing patterns of inequality. Digital platforms should serve members of marginalised communities who rely on them most and who are most vulnerable to exploitation.

Sixth, it fosters a culture of collaboration, solidarity and hope in which a spirit of innovation and invention is harnessed for socially useful ends. The problem-solving and tinkering culture which has long been part of the technology world can only be fully realised when technology is liberated from capitalism.[11] Collaboration towards shared goals rather than competition between profit-making firms should be the driving principle of the development of new technology. Our brightest minds should be empowered to work towards producing socially beneficial technology rather than solving narrow problems around generating revenue and increasing user engagement. We need a new sense of hope for the future to replace the current cynicism and pessimism about the future of technology.

In many respects, this proposal runs against the grain of contemporary criticism of digital platforms from the Left and Right. After 2016, with Trump's election, the Cambridge Analytica data breach scandal and growing awareness of the rampant exploitation of the gig economy, few would argue that digital platforms could help tackle society's problems. But without a belief in the possibility of a better future emancipatory politics becomes impossible. There is much that remains open and uncertain in our world. Nobody could have predicted the unforeseen changes that have occurred over the past decade. We require what Ernst Bloch calls *docta spes*, 'educated hope', a belief in the rich potential of our agency which has not yet been realised in the world. This does not mean we should adopt a naively optimistic standpoint or doubt the enormity of the task facing us. Our 'pessimism of the intellect' needs to be combined with a commitment to a future of mutual care, solidarity and collaboration based on our collective capacity for political action.

To achieve these goals, this book proposes a series of concrete institutional reforms to recode how the digital economy operates. The first level concerns the democratisation of the platform – individual platform companies should be opened up to the ideas and actions of their members through changes to their ownership and governance structures. After developing the principles of platform socialism through engagement with neglected figures from the socialist tradition, I examine four specific cases of a ride hail app, short-term rentals, an internet search engine and distributed social networks. These case studies range from the local and civic to the international, demonstrating how we could think about democratisation at different levels of complexity.

Our concern, however, is not only with questions of workplace democracy – how individual enterprises should be owned and managed – but with broader considerations of economic democracy concerning larger macro-level issues over the allocation of resources. The majority of the analysis in this book focuses on the platform economy rather than the tech industry as a whole or the broader economy. The world's largest digital platforms present an important case study of what is happening at the cutting edge of capitalist development. The largest and most profitable companies in the world are now mostly American tech companies. Their extraordinary concentration of power, immense profitability and wide-ranging effects on social life have made these firms particularly prominent in the public consciousness. The world of tech is where the American dream of rags to riches is still alive and well. The platform economy matters deeply both strategically and ideologically to capitalism, which is why it serves as an important site for democratic intervention. However, democratising digital platforms necessarily lead us to broader issues of how resources are allocated. I discuss a system of *participatory planning* as a way for us to deliberate over the best allocation of resources in a democratic and pluralist economy.

Our vision of the future needs to be accompanied by a plan for how to achieve it. Lasting change will never come about with benevolent Silicon Valley CEOs growing a conscience. A fundamental transformation of the platform economy will only be achieved through a shift in the balance of power between platform owners and the communities they exploit. Achieving this will require an analysis of the current balance of forces to understand how we can swing them in our favour. We need to pinpoint strategically vulnerable points to focus our energies and identify the types of reforms that would strengthen our position.

We are currently in a dire situation. Tech platforms have enormous power and opponents of digital platforms are deeply divided on the nature of the problem and how best to address it. We should be under no illusions about the difficult road ahead. Struggling against the power of the tech capitalist class will require transforming society from the bottom up and engaging in multiple and diverse struggles at different points in the system. Any kind of truly transformative project will take time and will require the gradual build up of oppositional forces.

The approach advocated here is a threefold strategy of *resisting, regulating* and *recoding* existing digital platforms.[12] First, we need to support bottom-up struggles that resist the power of Big Tech companies and the immediate harms they cause to workers and the broader community. Second, we should also call on states and transnational regulatory authorities to further enhance protections for workers and to properly enforce existing laws. Finally, we need to foster alternative systems and processes of collaborative production that could eventually come to replace these companies with democratic alternatives. These three strategies are complementary. Stronger regulations can enhance workers' bargaining power and catalyse more workers to join unions. Similarly, empowered social movements applying pressure from below can push governments to take bolder action in reining in Big Tech. A thriving ecosystem of well-established alternative models also weakens the power of major tech companies to control how we envision the future. We need to support existing movements against Big Tech that put forward radical demands and place questions of democracy, ownership and control at the centre of their organising.

This book is about how we can reimagine our relationship with digital platforms. It invites readers to consider how we can press the reset button on the drive to commodification and establish a radically new set of principles for our digital lives. Through the collective action of workers and platform users we need to build our power to fight back against Big Tech. My hope is that recognising the fragility of Big Tech's grasp on our future and the collective strength that exists in our communities might embolden us to strive for more radical alternatives to the status quo. We are now at a crossroads. The next ten years will prove decisive as to whether we can reclaim our digital future from the hands of tech billionaires or whether we will continue down a path of exploitation and domination. Whoever controls the platforms, controls the future. The simple proposition of this book is that this should be us.

1
All the World's a Platform

We live in a world where we are daily confronted by the possibilities and perils of the platform economy. There is a burgeoning ecosystem of platforms and apps that cater to our every need, from online shopping to domestic services, entertainment streaming and transportation. As we have grown accustomed to the contours of our new digital environment we have swung violently between tech utopianism and anxiety. The wondrous possibilities of technological mastery have been accompanied by fears of a loss of autonomy and the rise of a foreboding system of algorithmic domination. The tech-enabled utopia that flows from the pages of Big Tech's PR departments is full of luxury and convenience – where one's entire life can be seamlessly optimised on smart devices. Digital platforms promise us instant satisfaction and quick access to an array of consumer goods at our fingertips. Whether it's a burger, a ride or a home loan, there's an app that can take care of it. But they also appear inextricably enmeshed within new systems of surveillance and control. These two dimensions of the platform economy are interlinked. You can have convenience but at the cost of ceding control to a corporation. You can have private luxury but only through the erosion of public goods. You invite platforms in to help make your life better only for them to help themselves to your data as part of the service.

Platform hypers have lauded these new digital tools for their ability to solve problems of trust, search time and quality verification that have hindered person-to-person markets.[1] Critics have sought to show how every 'uber' has an 'unter' and that the freedom and flexibility of some relies on the precarity and dependence of others.[2] To receive your meal at the click of a button, somebody else must be on standby waiting for your order to arrive. In the realm of platform labour, there is the highly visible world of 'men on wheels' – the ride hail drivers and delivery riders – but there is also the hidden, and much larger, domain of cleaning, care work and other household services.[3] For a privileged few, almost anything can be streamed or delivered straight to your home. For the rest, their job is to label data, assemble products and deliver packages, all to ensure that no cracks appear in the smooth functioning of our automated future.

As platforms have proliferated, so too has their reach into society. Many platforms now provide essential services for billions of people across the globe. It is becoming apparent that digital platforms are extending further than the doorsteps of their businesses and the screens of our phones. They are changing the face of urban infrastructure, providing mass transport to cities, controlling access to information, facilitating public debate and influencing elections. Social media platforms have the power to deplatform the president of the United States and determine the effective limits of free speech through their content moderation policies.

Global platforms are in the business of *world building*. Platforms are not satisfied with vertical and horizontal monopolies. They wish to create the entire environment within which we live. The ultimate goal is to be the owner of an ecosystem of interconnected products and services that effortlessly extracts profit at every point of the system. Like water to the fish, the global platform aims to be the imperceptible medium that permeates our entire existence. It is not enough to be one of the competitors in the field, the global platform wants to own the club, the stadium, the league and the franchise rights for advertisers.

For some of these entrepreneurs, the world is not enough. Facebook's latest ambitions are to grow larger still. Mark Zuckerberg announced that, 'over the next five years or so ... we will effectively transition from people seeing us as primarily being a social media company to being a metaverse company'.[4] Set out in an influential essay by venture capitalist Matthew Ball, the 'metaverse' will be an expansive and immersive set of experiences spanning physical and virtual worlds with a fully functioning economy and the possibility of content being seamlessly transferred across different experiences. As Ball prophesises in his essay, 'the Metaverse will be a place in which proper empires are invested in and built, and where these richly capitalized businesses can fully own a customer, control APIs/data, unit economics, etc.'.[5]

Platform companies have found a way to be both everywhere and nowhere. If you want to subscribe, they're only a click away. But if you are looking for taxes, their headquarters are not in your country and most of their profits have been paid to a subsidiary company as a licencing fee. If you bring a legal case against them, you might find they do not exist in your jurisdiction and therefore have not been correctly served with legal documents.[6]

The coronavirus pandemic has seen the platform world sink deeper into our lives. The pandemic has created a new demand for a touch-free and virtual society. The risk posed by direct human contact has led us to rely on a host of new tech and analogue products to navigate urban landscapes transformed by the virus. For many people, it seemed like their daily routine in lockdown was just shuffling from one platform to the next. The isolation era has accelerated existing trends of technology adoption and rapidly brought forward aspects of a tech-enabled world that may have been years away if not for the pandemic.

As the public health crisis worsened, tech business was booming. The pandemic offered an opportunity for the tech companies to roll out their products on an unprecedented scale. This dependence on a host of new tech products led to an extraordinary 41.1 per cent rise in the wealth of tech billionaires from April to July 2020.[7] The pandemic has also been a PR win for the industry, allowing it to shift gears after a few difficult years following allegations of Cambridge Analytica, influencing the Trump election campaign and growing concerns about tech monopolies. Suddenly, the tech companies began to reposition themselves as 'digital first responders' who were uniquely placed to pitch in and help out with the crisis.[8] The pandemic has led to increased collaboration between government and Big Tech, which has placed tech companies at the centre of new forms of identity management and health data extraction that will be around long after the pandemic has subsided.

UNDERSTANDING WHAT PLATFORMS DO

If we imagine a platform as some kind of space to gather people and facilitate value exchanges, the idea of a platform business is not a new phenomenon. Consider a marketplace or a modern shopping complex. What we now refer to as the platform economy consists of digital platforms that use tech infrastructure to scale the amount of activity that can be facilitated on the platform and reduce transaction costs for users.

Platform owners claim their products are neutral spaces and that they merely provide an intermediary service to connect parties. This is only half true. Through the design and architecture of the platform, software developers play an active role not only in connecting parties but in shaping the conditions in which they operate. In this sense, the metaphor of a 'platform' – a flat surface upon which other activities can take place – is entirely misleading. Digital platforms are themselves complex environments that have been painstakingly developed to guide users towards actions that are profitable for the company. Alongside explicit policies that regulate how parties will interact and on what terms, digital architects have built online landscapes that encourage certain types of behaviour through a deep understanding of human psychology and motivations built up over decades of social psychology and marketing studies. The seemingly smooth and open online space is in fact a carefully designed gradated and stratified world with gentle slopes that guide users towards specific sets of behaviours. These new technologies of power embody a fixed set of power relations between platform owners and users, calling into question the idea of platforms as neutral mediums that facilitate connection and empower users.

The platform economy is full of tensions and contradictions. This is partly because there are so many types of platforms using a variety of business models.[9] From advertising platforms (Facebook, Google) to brokerage (Uber, Deliveroo), e-commerce (Amazon, Alibaba), streaming (Spotify, Netflix) and cloud platforms (Amazon Web Services, Microsoft Azura), platform companies make money in different ways. Not all technology companies make money solely (or at all) through the platform economy. For example, Apple owns the Mac App Store, an app distribution platform, but in 2020, 50 per cent of its total revenue worldwide was generated by iPhone sales.[10] There is also no clear distinction between a 'digital' or 'platform' economy and the rest of the economy. Platforms are boundary-defying and have developed complex ecosystems of goods and services across multiple industries. These can have wide-ranging effects on other parts of the economy. Uber not only affects the taxi industry but also the food delivery economy with its subsidiary, UberEats. Another example is Amazon, which has completely reshaped multiple industries and has altered everything from the high street to global supply chains and cloud computing.[11]

There are three distinctive features of platforms that can help us make sense of their emerging role.[12] The first concerns how platform owners and investors benefit from *rentier relations*. These have emerged through the platform's role as a digital intermediary that facilitates the value-creating activity of others. We could describe digital platform owners as rentierist because many of these platforms generate revenue through the ownership and control of the platform under conditions of limited competition that enables them to undertake traditional gatekeeper activities such as charging transaction and usage fees.[13] Data harvested on the platform also enables profit generation through advertising revenue even if the users themselves are not charged for the service. Platforms are designed primarily for value capture rather than facilitating efficient market outcomes. As digital intermediaries, platforms provide value by maintaining the platform and lowering transaction costs for participants, but their primary source of profit comes from capturing value generated by others. The success of platforms relies on their ability to maintain their dominant position as an intermediary, even long after the parties were in contact and could get by on their own. This form of profit making differs from traditional models of goods and services delivery and enables platform owners to profit from 'having' rather than 'doing'. As Brett Christophers has recently shown, this form of rentierism has always been a significant element of the capitalist economy, with many other forms of rentierism using land, natural resources, infrastructure and intellectual property.[14]

Second, platforms generate two opposing movements: the concentration of profit and the dispersion of risk and responsibility. If it were not for six technology companies (Facebook, Amazon, Apple, Netflix, Google, Microsoft – known as FAANGM), Wall Street's Standard and Poor's (S&P) 500 index would have been down 4.2 per cent in the first half of 2020, rather than setting a record gain of almost 5 per cent.[15] The six technology stocks were up more than 43 per cent, with Amazon alone recording US$5.3 billion in the second quarter and a gain of more than 70 per cent in its share value since the beginning of the year.[16] This is in stark contrast to many other areas of the economy which are stagnating or in decline. The market's reliance on these tech companies signals a growing concentration of profit making in a small sector of the economy. It's also astonishing how much of this wealth ends up in the pockets of a few billionaire founders. Zuckerberg owns 29.3 per cent of Facebook, while Elon Musk owns 20.7 per cent of Tesla. We talk about tech as if it were creating value for humanity, but the reality is that wealth from the platforms ends up trapped inside a few private bank accounts.

At the same time as they centralise profits for shareholders, platforms outsource labour to 'independent' contractors and service providers to externalise the traditional costs and risks of doing business. This is accompanied by a less direct form of governance, which keeps parties at arm's length to avoid the costs associated with either maintaining a permanent labour force or fixed assets such as holiday homes or a fleet of cars. By acting primarily as intermediaries and denying greater levels of responsibility for the services provided on the platform, these businesses have found new ways to benefit from social and commercial activities without assuming the burden of direct control. As Juliet Schor and Steven Vallas have argued:

> The platform firm retains authority over important functions – the allocation of tasks, collection of data, pricing of services, and of course collection of revenues – but it cedes control over others, such as the specification of work methods, control over work schedules, and the labor of performance evaluation.[17]

The independence certain labour platforms grant to workers is a double-edged sword. Many workers find the flexibility of platform work to be a genuine benefit. But this 'flexibility' is designed to enable the companies to avoid providing longstanding labour protections such as ensuring a minimum wage, holiday and sick pay and retirement income, and bearing the full costs of employment.[18] Platforms are able to externalise the risks associated with service delivery onto poorly paid and precarious workers. If there is a long wait time between jobs, damage to assets or bad behaviour from clients, these must all be dealt with by the worker.[19] They also risk the deactivation of their accounts if customers rate them poorly on the platform.

Despite this abdication of responsibility by platform owners, a wide network of service users and workers become dependent on the platform for their livelihoods and social interactions. However, there is no universal experience of platform workers – either one of entrepreneurship or precarity – since platform work tends to be hierarchically organised in ways that intersect with workers' existing positions within the labour market.[20] Research by Juliet Schor and her colleagues across multiple platforms revealed that Airbnb hosts tended to be the most satisfied, while Uber drivers reported the worst experiences with the platform.[21] Schor accounts for this differential experience based on how dependent workers were on the platform to provide for their basic needs. Drivers in the ride hail sector tended to be more dependent on the platform as their sole source of income and were therefore more vulnerable and precarious. Airbnb hosts, on the other hand, could be property owners leveraging an existing asset to earn a supplemental income with a good effort-to-earnings ratio. Despite their different experiences, a unifying theme was having to bear the main risks and responsibilities of operating on the platform.

Third, many platforms benefit from network effects which enable them to scale rapidly, dominate markets and gain a monopoly over their sector. Network effects occur when platforms achieve large numbers of users which help them improve the service and increase the value of the platform. Platforms also have a capacity to grow exponentially due to the reduced demand for infrastructure, stock and personnel. Companies in the platform economy have fought hard to become the 'default' platform for use in their industry. By capturing the market, platforms can make users feel like they could not live without the social and commercial benefits that accompany access to their network. Google, Facebook and Amazon have all achieved an effective monopoly which allows them to dictate terms of exchange to parties and charge high fees or unfavourable terms of service regarding ownership of data.

In addition to these three attributes of the Big Tech platforms, there are also striking differences between the firms. One key difference is in their payouts to shareholders. Between 2000 and 2019, Microsoft and Apple returned roughly US$759 billion to shareholders, while Amazon, Facebook and Alphabet did not pay any dividends.[22] Rodrigo Fernandez and colleagues hypothesise that this could be a result of the maturation of tech companies following a period of scaling up and acquiring a dominant position, which then places them in a position to reward shareholders.[23] They also believe that payments depend on the role of founder owners. Companies like Amazon and Facebook, in which the original founders still hold much greater sway than institutional investors and other shareholders, were less likely to pay generous shareholder dividends. A second major difference is in their investment in physical infrastructure. Alphabet invested large amounts of capital – between US$84 billion and US$98 billion – in data centres and other fixed value assets. Similarly, Amazon made investments in cloud infrastructure, logistics and warehousing totalling US$98 billion. This is in contrast to Microsoft, Apple and Facebook which have fixed assets of between US$37 billion and US$45 billion.[24]

THE HIDDEN DIMENSIONS OF DATA

Platform businesses focus on the collection and analysis of data as an essential aspect of how they create value.[25] By data in this context I mean information and characteristics that are collected from activity on the platform which are recorded and stored for later analysis and exploitation. Storing and analysing data requires material resources, including data centres and data scientists to extract useful information that can be used to optimise operations or sell insights to advertisers. Through collecting information about human activities as data, platforms are able to convert this activity into a useable commodity for generating profit.

Data has an allusive quality in the digital economy, sometimes appearing to be a raw material, at other points a commodity, or even a new form of capital.[26] Some commentators have understood data in this sense as 'the new oil' of the digital economy.[27] On the surface, it appears to be a valuable asset akin to a natural resource. But unlike oil – and other raw materials – data is always data *of* something. Far from a multi-purpose good that can be plugged into a range of machines, data is information about specific phenomena. Data collected by Amazon on the processes of its warehouse operations will not necessarily be valuable to another company. Nor is there a single way to convert data into a profitable commodity. The science needed to leverage data into a profitable good is complicated and messy. The pay-offs on particular bundles of data depend on a range of contextual factors and do not follow the simple pattern of oil extraction and refinement.[28] Finally, oil's value comes from the fact that it is a finite resource that is difficult to extract, while data will exist so long as there is human activity to be recorded and analysed.

Others have made similar points to this before,[29] but there is another negative consequence of this view of data which has received less attention. This danger is what I call *data commodity fetishism*: the perception of certain digital relationships between people (especially for communication and exchange) as having their value based not on the social relationships themselves but on the data they produce.[30] When we understand data as a natural resource we mystify the true source of its value in the human activity required to produce it. Inside the data centres lies the reified activity of human beings. A whole range of interactions from everyday life is captured as profitable material: food deliveries, rideshares, online orders of household goods, messages with friends and relatives, job applications, overseas travel and online learning. Many internet users now spend more than four hours online every day.[31] The more our lives are spent online, the more they can be appropriated through data relations.

Data is often thought of as an unclaimed good 'out there' in a digital *terra nullius* – an empty space in which tech entrepreneurs can assert their rights over this seemingly free resource. As users of platforms, we tend not to see data through the same proprietary lens as other tangible goods, which has enabled tech companies to establish unfavourable norms over who should own and control data flows in digital spaces. The fact that we sign our rights away in terms of service agreements is not surprising because as individuals there is little value in our personal data trove. It's in the collection and analysis of large quantities of data where value can be generated. As Salome Viljoen has argued, companies' data collection practices are 'primarily aimed at deriving population-level insights from data subjects' that can then be used to develop advertising products.[32]

What is often left out of the discussion is the underlying source of this new profitable commodity, which is for the most part human activity appropriated by companies for profit. Admittedly, not all of the data tech companies collect is of human activity, but in the advertising model of Facebook and Google it is primarily consumer-related insights that offer the most value. Platforms create an environment in which an ever-increasing amount of our social activity takes place in contexts that are ready-made for appropriation. This expands the horizon of potential exploitation across every facet of our social interactions and deep within our inner thoughts and feelings as expressed online.

Platforms are not without precedent, but the ease and seamlessness through which our sociality is captured by data relations should be a cause of great concern. Economic extraction was never limited to activities that took place behind factory walls. We know that capitalism relies as much on the activities of unwaged domestic workers as much as full-time waged employees and precarious workers. However, the infrastructure of digital platforms enables a new form of appropriation to extend throughout the whole domain of the social, converting our social activity into profit.

LIFE INSIDE THE DIGITAL FACTORY

An unlikely guide to current trends can be found in the writing of the Italian Autonomist Marxists of the 1970s and 1980s who witnessed some of the first changes of deindustrialisation and the rise of an information society. Writers and activists such as Mario Tronti, Mariarosa Dalla

Costa and Antonio Negri foresaw how capitalism would make increasing use of technology as a means of expropriating human life.

The most iconic image from this body of literature is the 'social factory', which as Tronti argued implied that 'all of society lives as a function of the factory and the factory extends its exclusive domination over all of society'.[33] The thesis of the social factory implies that it is not simply the factory but also social relations considered as an interconnected field of activity that become subordinated to the logic of capitalist exploitation. Negri expressed this through the idea that 'the whole society is placed at the disposal of profit'.[34]

The 'socialised worker' represented an attempt to redefine the nature of work under capitalism which was inclusive of the feminist, youth and student movements, representing a new potentiality of productive labour. The argument was developed by feminist scholar Mariarosa Dalla Costa, who focused attention on the hidden reproductive labour of housewives that was both appropriated by capital and also denied existence as true productive work.[35] She argued that reproductive labour undertaken primarily by women was essential to maintaining the system of capital accumulation. Even many leftists denied that women's work in the household constituted social production, despite its clear centrality to social life. In an introduction to Dalla Costa's work, feminist Marxist Selma James argued that behind the factory lay a new arena of political struggle:

> The community therefore is not an area of freedom and leisure auxiliary to the factory where by chance there happen to be women who are degraded as the personal servants of men. The community is the other half of capitalist organization the other area of hidden capitalist exploitation the other hidden source of surplus labor. It becomes increasingly regimented like a factory what Mariarosa calls a social factory where the costs and nature of transport, housing, medical care, education, police, are all points of struggle! And this social factory has as its pivot the woman in the home producing labor power as a commodity, and her struggle not to.[36]

What autonomist feminists saw clearly was that capital's logic was not bound exclusively to a system of wage labour and market commodities. By shifting attention to a broader field of social relations, Dalla Costa developed a new understanding of how human life was appropriated by capital.

Autonomist Marxists believed that appropriation was no longer limited to wage labour and the production of surplus value. It wasn't the individual worker understood as producer who was the focus but the community considered as a social collective. Capital must appropriate communicative activity and find ways to convert this knowledge to a commodity form. This perspective opens up a new field of inquiry into how social activity is appropriated by capital through information technologies. Living amid the ongoing deindustrialisation of Italy and the decline of the collective power of industrial workers, they foresaw how these new domains of communication and circulation were becoming major spheres of profit extraction. With digital platforms, these developments reach a new level of intensity and magnitude.

THE CAPITALISATION OF HUMAN LIFE

Platform companies have sought to provide the digital infrastructure upon which we conduct our social lives. Many of these platforms insert themselves into our lives as middlemen, financialising everyday interactions. The most recent wave of commodification is so pervasive because it is not just our personal data that is monetised but our very sociability and shared life together. The digital recording of even the most mundane activities such as going for a run, seeing a friend, chatting to family and taking a vacation can all be fed into a system that analyses every detail to package for advertisers.

In *Platform Capitalism*, Nick Srnicek places the rise of platform-based businesses in the context of a broader history of capitalist development since the 1970s.[37] Srnicek shows how data is central to this new platform economy and reveals the continuities between the operations of platform businesses and previous capitalist enterprises. He underlines that the transformations are a product of long-term trends and the result of intense competition and profit-seeking between businesses looking to find new streams of revenue. As the use of the internet expanded, the public's increasing use of digital platforms opened up a new domain for profit-making in which our online activity could be tracked and monetised.

What we are witnessing is less of an epochal shift and more an intensification of capitalism's central logic of commodifying human life. Capitalism has always appropriated human life: from the slave trade to colonialism, factory labour and the sex work industry. Digital platforms expand this operation through a new model of data extraction. This process reflects the history of capitalism in capturing progressively greater aspects of human life as market commodities. Karl Marx was one of the keenest observers of the contradictory impulses of modernisation through the constantly expanding global market. For Marx, the ceaseless striving for wealth in capitalism destroyed older ways of life and constantly revolutionised the forces of production, initiating the search for ever more sophisticated ways to generate profit. Marx argued that this dynamism distinguished the modern capitalist period from previous epochs and set off an inexorable process in which 'all fixed, fast-frozen relations ... are swept away' and 'all that is solid melts into air'.[38]

The ownership of the infrastructure that facilitates these new forms of social relations is increasingly concentrated in a few hands with value flowing up the chain to platform owners. Previously non-monetised interactions now fall into a larger sphere of data extraction. For example, by analysing the geolocation points on our phones, companies can discern important information about our daily movements which might reveal valuable insights to advertisers. Even when we don't see ourselves as engaged in meaningful action, incidental interactions become part of a larger network of data capture and monetisation.

This capitalisation of social life was already part of the neoliberal revolution of the 1980s, but new digital technologies have enabled capital to penetrate far deeper into our social lives and to develop more sophisticated instruments of capture and control. If the neoliberal revolution was to make us see every aspect of our lives through the logic of the market, the platform revolution enabled companies to capitalise on our social lives through new technologies of power.[39] In other words, the neoliberal economisation of all features of social life was followed by their digital surveillance and commodification.

Platform businesses are constantly striving for new frontiers of profit and ways they can further integrate their systems into our lives. We are coming close to a world in which you won't be able to rent a home, shop at your local store or enter urban spaces without a subscription to a platform.[40] Already, we cannot access our primary means of communication online without wading through a sea of advertising and subtle behaviour modification systems. With every passing day, entrepreneurs find new ways in which digital technology can offer us convenience at the cost of surveillance and control.

SURVEILLANCE CAPITALISM IS STILL CAPITALISM

This interpretation of platform capitalism as an intensification of the appropriation of human life for profit breaks with the orthodoxy of the most influential account of digital technology and capitalism offered by Shoshana Zuboff in *The Age of Surveillance Capitalism*.[41] This book describes the business model of companies like Facebook and Google as offering free digital services in exchange for the collection of users' personal data, which is analysed to predict and influence their behaviour through targeted advertising. Zuboff argues that this model represents a new economic order, a new form of power and a pivotal moment in the history of humanity. While the book provides important insights into the business model of advertising platforms, it obscures the extent to which the logic of surveillance capitalism is in fact a continuation of a logic of extraction and commodification inherent in capitalism itself.[42]

The book sets up a binary framework of 'surveillance capitalism' and 'advocacy-oriented capitalism'. Surveillance capitalism appears as an aberration, a Frankenstein-like transmutation, of what digital capitalism could have been. We don't hear much about advocacy-oriented capitalism in the text, but it represents an alternative pathway for informational societies. Advocacy-oriented firms seek to empower customers by advocating for their interests and aligning commercial operations to meet genuine consumer needs through reciprocal relationships. The implicit idea of the surveillance capitalism paradigm is that there is a healthy and advocacy-oriented capitalism to which we could potentially return.

The overlooked hero of Zuboff's text is an idealised version of Apple, which among the tech companies comes closest to embodying Zuboff's ideal customer-empowering model of enterprise.[43] At the same time as Google was stripping users' digital carcasses bare for behavioural surplus, Apple promised an advocacy-oriented digital capitalism. There is a sense in the book that if tech companies had all just made iPods we wouldn't be in this mess. The beauty of these high-margin physical products for Zuboff is that they satisfy consumer demand, align with what customers want and can be improved through feedback and competition to better satisfy customer needs. This leads to a virtuous cycle of consumers getting 'what I want, when I want, where I want' and companies making bucketloads of money. The advocacy model is characterised by 'the *behavioral value reinvestment cycle*, in which all behavioral data are reinvested in the improvement of the product or service'.[44] The core of the critique of surveillance capitalism is that this cycle is subverted by using behavioural surplus not to improve services but to create 'prediction products' and targeted advertising to control human behaviour.

However, when applied to the real world, the myth of a virtuous, well-functioning advocacy-oriented capitalism quickly breaks down. Zuboff lists a litany of Apple's negative externalities – practices which are common to many capitalist firms: 'extractive pricing policies, offshoring jobs, exploiting its retail staff, abrogating responsibility for factory conditions, colluding to depress wages via illicit noncompete agreements in employee recruitment, institutionalized tax evasion, and a lack of environmental stewardship'.[45] Instead of understanding these as logical outcomes of a highly competitive company, these practices are depicted as curious states of exception 'that seemed to negate the implicit social contract of its own unique logic'.[46] Apple's advocacy-oriented model is claimed to have been 'poorly understood: a mystery even to itself', as if the company only needed to better understand what it truly was.[47]

At the centre of Zuboff's theory stands the sovereign individual consumer who demands 'my life, my way, at a price I can afford'. The ideal company is the one that can adequately satisfy these demands. Forms of collective action and solidarity appear only as a means to ensure the sovereign consumer gets what she wants. Insofar as it stands as a critique of digital capitalism, Zuboff's book is limited in its scope to the business model of advertising platforms and has little to say about other forms of exploitation in the digital economy. The overarching framework of 'behavioural surplus = bad/service improvement = good' misses the ways in which an extractive business model that commodifies human life is at the heart of both industrial and digital capitalism. When this schema is turned to other tech companies the distinction begins to break down. To what extent does Uber's use of consumer data to improve its service constitute a form of advocacy-oriented capitalism? What if they used the data to aggressively push out competitors, underpay workers and control drivers' behaviour? Is this just advocacy-oriented capitalism gone wrong or would it constitute full-blown surveillance capitalism? The problem lies in the fact that the text is unaware of how broader aspects of the critique of surveillance capitalism could be applied to capitalism itself. The problem with surveillance capitalism is not simply the new techniques of surveillance but the competitive capitalist economy that drives them.

REPURPOSING TECHNOLOGY

The growing omnipresence of these platforms at every point of our lives first appears as a source of their power and as an impediment to challenging their dominance. How could we hope to fight the very network within which we live? From another angle, however, this could also be seen as a vulnerability. Tech companies are fundamentally reliant on our activity as the source of their valuable enterprises. It's our lives, our labour, our creativity, our tools and our assets that make them money. Their function is more value capture than value creation. Without us, their companies cease to exist. They own the data centres, the software and the equipment, but we are the hamster in the wheel that keeps the whole machine running.

In some respects, the situation is not so different from industrial-era capitalism. Marx was fond of gothic imagery. He imagined capital as 'dead labour, which, vampire-like, lives only by sucking living labour, and lives the more, the more labour it sucks'.[48] One of the most striking metaphors of his writing was of capital as a lifeless vampiric force that was fundamentally dependent on the power of workers.[49] This metaphor paints the capitalist class as an unproductive and superfluous entity that could be removed from the process altogether. It is a reminder that we have the power to reclaim the ownership and control over technology and to repurpose it for our own use. Following the analysis of two platform companies – Facebook and Airbnb – in Chapters 2 and 3, the second half of the book shows how this transformation could be achieved in practice.

All the world's a platform, and all the men and women are merely users. By setting the stage and charging for tickets, tech entrepreneurs manage a show in which we are both unpaid actors and swindled audience members in our own production. Let's take back the theatre, rewrite the script and put on the performance of our lives.

2
Monetising Community

A quiver of excitement and anticipation ripples through the air as the crowd awaits the speaker for the main event. People are sitting in a tightly packed hall in downtown Chicago. This is the birthplace of community organising. This is where Saul Alinsky first founded the Back of the Yards Neighborhood Council in the 1930s and where Barack Obama spent his formative years as a grassroots organiser.[1] Suddenly, the low-key background music cuts out and generic upbeat corporate music blasts through the speakers. Everyone rises to their feet, cheering enthusiastically. The room is illuminated with the glow of mobile phone screens as people try to capture the historic moment.

Mark Zuckerberg begins to make his way to the front of the room, taking his time glad-handing members of the crowd. He gradually emerges from his carefully curated community of supporters, 'good to see you … good to see you … good to see you', and then suddenly, 'I can't take this anymore, I'm going up on stage'.[2] The music fades and the assembled Facebook group admins begin whooping as Zuckerberg thanks the audience and prepares to give his address. It's 22 June 2017, the first ever Facebook Communities Summit. Mark Zuckerberg will announce a change to Facebook's mission statement, setting the company on a new course for the next decade. If you wanted to pick a moment for the emergence of a new understanding of the role of community in the platform economy this would be it.

This event is about communities, big and small. It's scheduled at a watershed moment when the Facebook community is about to reach two billion members. The event will recognise the many small communities within Facebook that support people and give them a sense of meaning and purpose. It turns out that Mark, as he winsomely refers to himself, is also a member of a number of tight-knit digital communities. Today is not about the billionaire CEO and tech entrepreneur but the family man, community member and non-threatening geek.

Mark is a member of the 'Zuckerberg family group' and 'Max's Circle', which he describes as 'like our family group except we all just share cute photos of my daughter doing ridiculous things'. An image of his baby dressed as Obi Wan Kenobi flashes up on screen and is predictably adorable. Zuckerberg is also a member of five different groups dedicated to a Hungarian breed of dog called the Puli. This is his family pet, 'basically a walking mop, but instead of making things cleaner he makes things dirtier'. He announces he is also the admin of 'a group for people who like playing the game Civilization', with 52 members. The tagline of the game, 'build an empire to stand the test of time', may prove more prescient for Zuckerberg himself than any of the historical figures featured in the game. Alongside Zuckerberg there are dozens of other regular folk playing their part in the patchwork of communities that make up Facebook's groups.

After deep reflection on his experience 'connecting the entire world', Zuckerberg announces a paradigm shift for Facebook: from group to community and from connection to belonging. 'It's not enough to simply connect the world, we must also work to bring the world closer together. ... Communities give us that sense that we are part of something bigger than ourselves, that we are not alone, that we have something better ahead to work for.'[3] These were not necessarily communities of place based on geographical location but online communities in which people still felt a sense of common interest and shared purpose.

Facebook's success as a business owes much to the way in which it established proprietary rights over a social commons embedded in online communities. The business model could be understood as an enclosure of this commons based on a parasitic relationship in which Facebook's owners capture value created by its users. Facebook both sells itself as a space for communities and also relies on communities as one of its primary sources of value. At the time of its creation, none of this was apparent to either the creator or initial users of Facebook's service.

It's painfully clear that as a young student writing code for his new website, Thefacebook, in January 2004, Zuckerberg had no idea about the social forces he would unleash on the world. He had no skills in community building and only a limited understanding of the sociological phenomena that were developing through his social network. Intense and introverted as a child, Zuckerberg spent endless hours coding with the support of a software developer his parents hired to give him private lessons. His 13-year journey of discovery in which he reinvented the purpose of Facebook provides insight into the changing nature of how we think about digital community.[4]

BUILDING A SENSE OF PURPOSE

Zuckerberg started out with an idea which is still prevalent today – we could call it a 'social network as database' model of thinking. The platform is a network connecting different nodes, and people's posts and interactions provide the input for the collection of data. In 2005, he thought of Facebook as 'an online directory' that could be used 'to look people up and find information about people'.[5] Later, Zuckerberg recounted how he used to think of Facebook as 'a living database of all of this content and the stories of people's lives. ... And, just like any database, you should be able to query it. ... We imagine that every screen of the Facebook product is the result of some query that someone is doing to learn something about their network and the people around them'.[6] For young Zuckerberg, Facebook was an information bank that contained publicly available and searchable data on people's lives.

The picture for this way of thinking was the social graph: a diagrammatic representation of a social network in which people are depicted as nodes and their relationships as lines called 'edges'. It was a way of codifying social relations according to a 2000s mindset, creating a global map of everybody and how they were related. 'The social graph is changing the way the world works', Zuckerberg said at a conference in 2007. 'We are at a time in history when more information is available and people are more connected than they ever have been before, and the social graph is at the centre of that.'[7] Facebook's value was in its capacity to provide access to a wide variety of data on a range of people. Technology was able to create a useable database and provide 'a mirror for the real community that existed in the real life'.[8]

In the beginning, the social mission was about transparency. Zuckerberg described sitting with his Harvard roommates, Chris Hughes and Dustin Moskovitz: 'we'd talk about how we thought that the added transparency in the world, all the added access to information and sharing would inevitably change big-world things. But we had no idea we would play a part in it. ... We were just a group of college kids.'[9] Information freely provided by people about their lives was the engine of this system and provided the fuel for the growth of the platform. The social graph, it was hoped, would make access to information easier and provide a community asset through which data could be used for social good.

The problem with this model was that the graph was two dimensional and only provided a superficial understanding of the network. It lacked depth, content and most of all meaning. It could answer questions about 'who' and 'how' but lacked any insight into 'why'. In 2016, a new phrase entered Zuckerberg's vocabulary: *meaningful communities* – 'these are groups that upon joining, quickly become the most important part of our social network experience and an important part of our physical support structure'.[10]

The model of the database required a sociologically richer account of why people used the network and what value they derived from it. It required an understanding of individuals' sense of purpose and how this was connected to a larger idea of building community. Facebook wasn't a simple database but a tool for people to share experiences, support each other and solve collective challenges. Its users were not an anonymous network but were woven into a rich tapestry of a global community consisting of millions of subcommunities such as sporting groups, student dorms and fan clubs.

Following the political upheavals of 2016, Zuckerberg began to understand Facebook's own purpose in epochal terms: 'We're at this next point in human civilization, where we have the next set of tools that we need, things like the internet, that can be this global communication infrastructure. ... Just like we went from hunter-gatherers to villages and cities and then nations, I think we now need to come together as a global community'.[11]

Facebook was now an essential player in a world-historical process of building global community through its infrastructure and tools. No longer merely a repository of information, the platform took centre stage as a political actor in the long march of civilisational progress. Channelling Martin Luther King Jr, Zuckerberg declared, 'the great arc of human history bends toward people coming together in ever greater numbers – from tribes to cities to nations – to achieve things we couldn't on our own'.[12] Facebook had become a key battleground for electoral parties and a source of political information for citizens. Zuckerberg imagined it playing a decisively political role: 'this is the struggle of our time. The forces of freedom, openness, and global community against the forces of authoritarianism, isolationism, and nationalism'.[13]

Its mission was to connect people through the platform and provide them with tools to join meaningful communities. Zuckerberg began to provide a more developed vision of Facebook's potential as providing the 'social infrastructure' of online communities which would help individ-

uals to meet a variety of their 'personal, emotional and spiritual needs'.
Communities were shown to

> provide all of us with a sense of purpose and hope; moral valida-
> tion that we are needed and part of something bigger than ourselves;
> comfort that we are not alone and a community is looking out for us;
> mentorship, guidance and personal development; a safety net; values,
> cultural norms and accountability; social gatherings, rituals and a way
> to meet new people; and a way to pass time.[14]

The goal, for Zuckerberg, was 'to strengthen existing communities by
helping us come together online as well as offline ... we reinforce our
physical communities by bringing us together in person to support each
other'.[15] Ultimately, 'Facebook stands for bringing us closer together and
building a global community'.[16]

SCROLLING ALONE

What's interesting about this new paradigm is how it draws on a familiar
theme of a longing for lost community that appears again and again
in political writing throughout the modern period. In *The Inoperative
Community*, French philosopher Jean Luc Nancy describes how this consciousness of a lost community has structured Western thought:

> The lost, or broken, community can be exemplified in all kinds of
> ways, by all kinds of paradigms; the natural family, the Athenian
> city, the Roman Republic, the first Christian community, corpora-
> tions, communes, or brotherhoods – always it is a matter of a lost age
> in which community was woven of tight, harmonious and infrangi-
> ble bonds and in which above all it played back to itself, through its
> institutions, its rituals, and its symbols, *the* representation, indeed the
> living offering, of its own immanent unity, intimacy, and autonomy.[17]

There is a recurring refrain of the dangers of rampant divisions and the
need for a return to a lost unity and harmony. Each generation has its
own version of this loss of community, projected back into the near past
– an imagined time in which neighbours greeted each other and kids
gathered in safe streets to go fishing in nearby unpolluted lakes.

The most recent iteration of the decline of community thesis was articulated in *Bowling Alone*, a bestselling book published in 2000 by Harvard professor Robert Putnam. Putnam's thesis was that since the 1960s American society had experienced a steady drop in membership of civic associations, which resulted in reduced civic engagement and social capital.[18] This included a decline in national turnout for elections, attendance of public meetings and town halls, religious affiliation, union membership, parent–teacher associations, volunteering in various civic associations and – as the title of the book suggests – participation in league bowling clubs. Sociologists have disputed whether the study misses other forms of engagement and social interaction not picked up by Putnam's metrics, but the popularity of his book is indicative of the widespread view of a growing sense of social dislocation occurring over the past decades.

This sense of communities in decline began to be felt more acutely in the 1980s and 1990s than in previous decades due to the effects of neoliberal economic policies that eroded community cohesion and membership of social organisations. In the 1970s, the Fordist model of capitalism went into crisis resulting in the rise of finance capital and a restructuring of the production process, with the relocation of many industrial activities to peripheral countries in the global economy.[19] Deindustrialisation resulted in factory and mine closures, job losses and communities left without sufficient social and economic support.

The neoliberal consensus of the 1980s favoured economic liberalisation, deregulation, privatisation and the expansion of free markets. It also aimed to disrupt social collectives like trade unions and sought to depoliticise political struggles. In their place, neoliberals promoted an ideology of personal responsibility and a host of market-based solutions to individuals' problems. For generation Xs and millennials who grew up during this period, traditional 'institutional' forms of community such as unions, political parties, places of worship, civic associations and social clubs were on the decline, replaced by smaller 'tribes' of friends (epitomised by 1990s TV shows like *Friends* and *Seinfeld*). Putnam's research found a receptive audience because the evidence for his thesis was everywhere.

In a 2017 open letter entitled 'Building Global Communities', Zuckerberg offered his own take on this theme, which positioned Facebook as offering a potential solution to these social problems. For Zuckerberg, the weakening of social ties began to occur half a century ago:

there has been a striking decline in the important social infrastructure of local communities over the past few decades. Since the 1970s, membership in some local groups has declined by as much as one-quarter, cutting across all segments of the population. The decline raises deeper questions alongside surveys showing large percentages of our population lack a sense of hope for the future. It is possible many of our challenges are at least as much social as they are economic – related to a lack of community and connection to something greater than ourselves.[20]

Both Putnam and Zuckerberg diagnose the loss of community as a distinctive problem for our time and argue that we need to find new pathways to restore social connection and a sense of belonging. Facebook's mission was to provide its own digital infrastructure and tools to support online communities, which have the potential to 'strengthen existing physical communities' and 'enable completely new ones to form'. In the wake of a decline of social capital and meaningful relationships, Facebook could step in to fill the gap. Rather than a harbinger of these new forms of alienation and isolation, Facebook was ideally situated to resolve them: 'in a world where this physical social infrastructure has been declining, we have a real opportunity to help strengthen these communities and the social fabric of our society'.[21]

COMMUNITY AND CAPITALISM

There is a deep irony in one of the world's most successful entrepreneurs portraying his company as a champion of grassroots community. Throughout its long history, the growth of capitalism has led to the disintegration of communities across the globe and the destruction of traditional ways of life. It seems we have now reached a time at which the very forces responsible for the erosion of community are now attempting to sell it back to us in a monetised form.

Community and capitalism are becoming increasingly entwined in a new relationship through digital technology. Notions of community are at the heart of the practices and rhetoric of many of the latest generation of platform companies. Tech companies have come to see community as a new domain of profitable extraction. Companies profit from our longing for traditional forms of community by stepping into a space left open by globalisation and social disconnection. Community is such a powerful marketing tool because it taps into one of our deepest sources of meaning.

Platform companies attempt to cultivate communities of users on their platform in order to extract profit from them. Facebook draws on the fundamental human motivation of seeking out a sense of belonging through the promotion of its groups and communities as a way of attracting and retaining users.[22] Belonging is more than just connection, it entails a deeper sense of significance and meaning. We desire not simply to share information but to be a part of a collective and participate in something bigger than ourselves. Social media might fulfil this purpose imperfectly, but following the decline of real-world communities, it is increasingly a place where people seek out these relationships. Throughout their history, companies such as Airbnb, eBay and TaskRabbit have also utilised a sense of a community of users to motivate people to use their platform and maintain an emotional connection with the service.

In industrial capitalism, human labour power was exploited to generate surplus value through wage labour. In the platform economy, this exploitation is combined with new socio-technical systems that capture and control the bonds of community itself and extract informational resources from them. This leads to a loss of community as a space in which people can come together for free and open dialogue and an experience of collective self-determination. In its place emerges a new kind of enclosed digital community in which connection with others is mediated through corporate digital architecture.

THE ADVERTISING MODEL

The turn to community acknowledges that the real source of value for a company like Facebook lies not in its data, digital infrastructure or software but in the social activities of its members. As of June 2021, Facebook had a market capitalisation of US$936.41 billion, but the people who are most integral to its success share in none of this wealth.[23] To understand why this is the case, we need to take a closer look at its business model and examine how value is created and captured by the platform.

Facebook had more than 2.85 billion monthly users in the first quarter of 2021, with a 10 per cent rise from the previous year.[24] The average user spends 38 minutes a day using the service. More than 1.4 billion people use Facebook Groups each month, which hosts more than 10 million user-administered groups for people to 'build a community around shared expertise, passions, beliefs, and situations'.[25] These large figures matter a lot for the business because they ensure Facebook's hegemony in the social media landscape and help to attract new users to the service.

Facebook's business is a low-cost, high-profit, money-making machine, with the company reporting US$25.44 billion in advertising revenue (97.2 per cent of total revenue) in the first quarter of 2021, up 46 per cent from the same quarter in the previous year.[26] It has basically no marketing costs, limited transaction costs and no costs on units (of advertising) sold. Despite a high-profile advertiser boycott in July 2020, Facebook's profits continued to soar during the Covid-19 pandemic, with an 11 per cent year-on-year increase in revenue to US$18.69 billion in the second quarter of 2020.[27]

The advertising model Facebook employs is now generally well understood – individuals use the service free of charge in exchange for their data being collected, analysed and sold to third-party companies for the purposes of targeted advertising. The underlying premise is not so different from twentieth-century marketing: companies want to know as much information as possible about potential customers to create advertising products. The innovation of digital platforms is in their enhanced ability to understand consumer behaviour and preferences and therefore create advertising products able to narrow in on very particular segments of the market. They are also assisted by the infrastructure of programmatic advertising that automates the selling of ads and holds real-time auctions as webpages load.[28]

Many of us might assume that Facebook's model of 'free service for targeted ads' is a reasonably fair exchange and that users willingly accept this. After all, despite all the hate, Facebook is enormously popular and its users greatly benefit from the wide range of opportunities it affords them. It would strike many as odd to call users 'exploited' in any meaningful sense of the term. They voluntarily agree to use the service and there is no economic compulsion to remain on the platform. Concerns have been raised about potential privacy breaches like Cambridge Analytica – but with sufficient regulation and oversight, platforms like Facebook are widely considered to be useful tools for billions of people across the globe.

Considered more closely, we have good reason to believe that this widely accepted view is wrong because it fails to consider the injustice of the unchecked structural power imbalances that have accrued to platform owners. We've been forced to accept the concentration of an oligarchic ownership structure and the flows of value from the bottom to the top as the only way the platform could operate. This extractive model has been naturalised as a seemingly necessary aspect of this new technology. Facebook provides the paradigmatic model of a business that feeds off its users in order to generate billions in shareholder value, which is hoarded by a tiny minority of investors. What is often overlooked is how much it relies on its users' activity as the true source of the company's value. Facebook creates the products, but there is nothing sacred about these digital tools that couldn't be replicated and operated for the benefit of all. The constant push to optimise for growth and engagement could be replaced with a different set of values which could guide how the technology could be developed.

Facebook has built much hype around revolutionising social connections and how people participate in the public sphere. But we should be wary of celebratory accounts of the participatory nature of web 2.0 that focus on cultural phenomena without interrogating the underlying economic relations between new social actors.[29] If we examine Facebook from a political economy perspective a very different picture emerges.

HOW FACEBOOK EXPLOITS ITS USERS

To exploit someone is to take unfair advantage of them and use them for your benefit.[30] Most people would not see social media platforms as exploiting their users in this way.[31] If we are to make the case for Facebook exploiting its users in a morally relevant sense, it cannot be according to the same model as salaried employees or contracted labourers. Facebook's users are clearly not exploited in the same manner as cobalt miners in the Democratic Republic of Congo, assembly workers in China's special economic zones or Facebook's employees working in California. Many would agree that the first and second categories are exploited, while socialists argue that even the third is exploited in the sense that the value workers create for the company is extracted by its owners in exchange for a wage less than the value they produce.[32] The exploitation of user-generated content is by no means the most egregious form of exploitation, but it is one that is still often misunderstood and for which we don't yet have a standard vocabulary. This argument returns to the 'free labour' debates among early critical theorists of the web and provides an alternative account of why there is still exploitation even in the absence of activity that would fit within a Marxist theory of labour.[33]

The claim here is that the power structure of social media platforms creates a distinct form of exploitation that can be distinguished from the classical Marxist definition and other forms of the exploitation of labour that occur within the platform economy. I call this form of exploitation 'user-generated profit', which involves the transfer of value from a subordinated productive group of users to largely unproductive platform owners and investors who benefit from users' activity. In the definition adopted here, Facebook exploits its community of users because it takes unfair advantage of a structural power asymmetry between owner and user in order to extract economic benefit from them.

Facebook actively promotes its service as a means for people to maintain relationships and build communities. The social network site capitalises on the social interactions of its users, with 88 per cent of users reporting they use the service to connect with friends and family.[34] The value produced in these exchanges of information is irreducible to any single user of the service. It is the community as a whole which is the source of value for the company and which creates the affective bonds that attract new users and retain existing ones.

This is not Marx's account of industrial capitalism's exploitation of labour power through a system of wage labour, but there are certain parallels. Capitalists have power over workers because workers require a wage to live. They don't have to work for any particular employer, but they do have to work for somebody. Capitalists exercise structural power over workers because they have something workers need and are the only ones who can give it to them. Without a wage workers would become destitute.

In our era, traditional forms of community have in many respects been eroded. Online social networks like Facebook, Instagram and Twitter are where many people go to interact with others and feel a sense of connection. The largest of the global networks exercise a near monopoly over this resource because they have so many users. The vast number of users and the global reach is what makes the networks so valuable. There are of course avenues to pursue community in real life and on other networks online, but the dominant position of a few tech companies cannot be denied. We could also note that there is a significant minority who don't use social networks and seem to get along just fine. But this doesn't change the fact that a majority of people with access to the internet feel that these networks are valuable enough to become members and that one of their primary uses is to access community.

Social reproduction theorists such as Tithi Bhattacharya ask, 'what kinds of processes enable the worker to arrive at the doors of her place of work every day so that she can produce the wealth of society?'[35] They point to the processes of care, education and reproductive labour that facilitate workers being able to do their job. In a similar manner, we could inquire as to what social and communal needs workers have that must be fulfilled in order to lead fully human lives and achieve a sense of belonging and connection with others. In our fragmented and dislocated world it is increasingly tech companies that claim ownership over the social infrastructure of twenty-first century community.

The parallel with workers under capitalism is that a dominant class controls access to a resource that is difficult to obtain elsewhere. If you are not on Facebook and other social networking sites, it's likely that you are won't have access to important social and professional networks. There are four main elements of the definition that require further explanation: a lack of coercion, an unequal exchange of economic benefit, a structural power asymmetry and taking advantage unfairly.

EXPLOITATION WITHOUT COERCION

First, we need to explain why a free service which we are not compelled to use should be considered exploitative. We can speak of an 'exploitation without coercion' to define this less direct form of the appropriation of value which does not require platform owners to exercise direct supervision and control over the exploited group. One of the key characteristics of platforms is that they enable the extraction of economic value from transactions and interactions without the added responsibility of directly controlling them. While people may be surveilled and recorded more than ever, they are also relatively free to do as they like. Unlike the tightly organised regime of factory and workplace discipline, Facebook's users are encouraged to log on whenever they want, create freely and exercise complete control over their activity.

While they are forced to use a particular protocol on the site and adhere to certain 'community standards' (set unilaterally by Facebook), in theory they can use the network as often or as little as they want. But by virtue of their ubiquity and dominance certain platforms have achieved a monopoly position which encourages users to participate due to the economic and social benefits of the platform. Many individuals feel that a network such as Facebook offers a valuable resource (access to the network) that would cause them social and economic hardship to do without. As the platform economy becomes ever more central to social life, it becomes harder to see these networks as just some of the options from which an individual could freely choose.

WHERE IS THE HARM?

Second, we need to explain why this exploitation seemingly causes no harm. This form of exploitation appears to benefit users and cost them nothing in return. It's a positive-sum transaction from which both platform owner and user gain something through a mutually consensual and beneficial transaction. For many commentators, the fact that Facebook is free and users seem to enjoy using it is enough to refute any argument that it is exploitative. However, the exploitation lies not in the causing of harm but in the taking advantage of a structural power asymmetry through organising an unequal exchange that disproportionately benefits the dominant party based on the activities of a subordinate group. Exploitation theory has typically focused on just these types of situations: positive-sum interactions that produce surplus for both parties.[36] The point is not that users would be unhappy with their experience but that their activity – often unknowingly – is instrumentalised for the creation of value for the dominant class.

Marx's account of the exploitation of labour power alludes to the worker performing 'unpaid labour' and 'working *gratis* for the capitalist'.[37] For Marx, the working day is spent partially on a worker's own subsistence and partially producing for the capitalist in the form of surplus value. This is an unequal exchange because there is an unreciprocated net transfer of value from a subordinate class to a dominant one. Marx paints the capitalist class as parasitic insofar as they live off the work of others. The working class produces all the value in society, but under capitalism it only receives a small fraction of this value back through wages. There is a similar form of freeloading going on in this example from the platform economy. Having developed the software and established themselves as dominant in the market, Facebook's owners add little independent value to the platform. The primary value-creating activity is user-generated content which is appropriated for profit.

WHO HAS THE POWER?

Third, Facebook's platform establishes an economic structure and a set of power relations between different agents through which economic resources are produced and distributed within the network. Ownership and control over the platform is vested in Facebook's original creators, senior management team and other investors. Users who want access to the network must adhere to the terms of service set out by Facebook in order to register an account.

The ubiquity of the platform and its penetration into so many aspects of our daily lives provides its owners with gatekeeper powers over any individual or business who wants access to the resources available in the network. In practice, the only option users have is to accept the terms of service offered by the platform owners or not to use the service. This structural power asymmetry benefits the owners and allows them to set unfavourable conditions on the use of the platform.

Social media platforms give rise to new digital hierarchies between those who exercise control and decision-making power over platform architecture, protocols and rules and those who must submit to these conditions. The most defining feature of this distinction is the economic advantage that platform owners receive from their capacity to monetise user-generated content and define the terms on which others can access the platform. At the basis of the structure lies the affective relations of Facebook's communities. It is undeniable that the creation of user-generated content is the most important source of value for the company, without which they would not be profitable. This value which is exploited is a result of network effects of the community and is irreducible to any single user. It is theoretically possible to quantify the average revenue per user, which differs significantly across regions. The appropriation of a user's activity is not uniform and cannot be measured by time expended or quantification of effort. The complexity of this process of commodification and exploitation makes it difficult to quantify in ways that highlight the contribution of any single node in the network. This reinforces the position that Facebook's users are exploited as a group and the process of value capture can only be properly understood at the level of the network.

ENCLOSING THE COMMONS

Fourth, Facebook's taking unfair advantage of its users can only be fully understood in the historical context of the commodification of the internet and the enclosure of this digital commons for private gain. We take it for granted that platform owners have a right to the economic benefits of commodifying this data because this is how the technology was introduced to us before the profitability of monetising user activity was widely understood. There is nothing normal or natural about the fact that digital platforms used by half the world should capture data that is then owned and exploited by a tiny minority. Zuckerberg himself as a single individual owns 28.2 per cent of the company and 88.1 per cent of its class B shares (which each have ten votes at the annual meeting).[38] This provides him with near total control over important decisions about the direction of the company.

Facebook did not invent message boards, community forums or social networks. Zuckerberg designed a simple, user-friendly and attractive model at a moment when the idea's time had come. It exploded because it was intuitive for its generation and tapped into what people were already starting to do across the country. When the network first caught on at Harvard, a 19-year-old Zuckerberg expressed disbelief that so many people, whom he kindly described as 'dumb fucks', would freely hand over their personal data. At the time it was introduced, people were unaware of the wealth that could be accumulated from such a data trove.[39] The business model and the extent of the data gathered was unprecedented.

However, Facebook's social network was built on the back of an enormous public investment of money in the digital infrastructure of the internet and continues to increase its profits from user-generated content supplied by its community of users. From its beginnings in ARPANET (the Advanced Research Projects Agency Network), funded by the US Department of Defense, the internet was developed through public investment in the military and university sectors. But due to the corporate-dominated policy-making and neoliberal political culture of the 1990s, the internet was quickly dominated by companies for the purpose of capital accumulation.

There is a historical analogy between the early capitalist enclosure of the commons and the digital enclosure of the internet by venture capitalists. The original movement was initially brought about in Europe through the enclosure of the commons – expelling peasants who would then form a landless proletariat – and the development of industrial centres of production in modern cities. Marx used the term primitive accumulation, referring to the dispossession of peasants from their land

and their entrance into labour markets as landless workers. In *Capital*, Marx described how the old English institution of communal property was gradually eroded with help from what Marx described as a 'parliamentary form of robbery': the Enclosure Acts, which granted landlords private ownership over land previously belonging to the people in common.[40] For centuries, English peasants depended on rights over common and waste land for planting crops, grazing animals, gathering wood and foraging for food. Small-scale agriculture of this kind was no utopia, but it maintained a relative degree of equality by sustaining self-sufficient rural life.

Enclosures occurred during two main periods in the sixteenth century and late eighteenth to early nineteenth centuries, with over 5,300 enclosure bills enacted between 1604 and 1914 relating to 6.8 million acres – over a fifth of the total area of England.[41] The term enclosure, understood in its more literal sense, refers to physically shutting off land through a wall or fence so that other cannot access it. But the historical and legal process entails something slightly different. It was not about whether land was fenced or open but about rights of ownership and access. The process of enclosure was concerned primarily with the removal of communal rights and ownership over land. This was referred to as its conversion into 'severalty', a status in which an owner exercised control over its use. This change in the law determined whether it was held 'in common' or owned privately. The periods of enclosure were about the conversion of public goods such that they could be redistributed as private assets.

In the case of the digital sphere, Facebook claims ownership over the data produced from the daily interactions of our social lives. This data, which is co-created by communities of individuals on the social network, becomes the exclusive property of Facebook to be analysed and sold as advertising commodities. Facebook takes unfair advantage of their position by capturing this resource from a digital commons. At the time of the digital enclosure, the loss of public goods that would occur was not immediately obvious. But as these networks have grown within a privatised system of commodification, the extent of the theft is becoming more apparent. Although today it would be harder for users to argue that they are unaware of the real trade that is being made in logging on to Facebook, the enclosure of a resource created by the activity of communities is a background condition that, in conjunction with the other factors mentioned above, demonstrates the exploitative nature of Facebook's business model.

My point here is not simply to bemoan the evils of a particular group of parasitic businesses but rather to lay the groundwork for a reconsideration of how digital platforms could be owned and operated. Platforms themselves are not capitalist or exploitative by nature; it was their development within a capitalist society and by people who sought to maximise their own profit that led to this position. Platforms could be socially owned, with the resources they create used to benefit all. We need to make the case for the democratic ownership and control of these platforms and show how we could build an alternative to today's exploitative digital economy.

3
Community-Washing Big Tech

Silicon Valley welcomes you to another of its 'community events', this time in San Francisco in March of 2017. Instead of picnic rugs, stalls and colourful bunting, we're treated to another tech CEO on stage in jeans and a designer T-shirt. Brian Chesky, one of three co-founders and CEO of Airbnb, is a former bodybuilder and cuts an impressive figure as he speaks energetically to the room. He's been described as audacious, idealistic and a travel revolutionary. Think of him as the Che Guevara of the short-term rental market.

Unlike other tech founders, Chesky wasn't a software engineer and knew little about tech or business before he started his 'home-sharing' website. He went to the Rhode Island School of Design where he learnt that 'you can redesign everything around you ... you can change the world'.[1] He is one of a number of tech billionaires who see themselves as the natural leaders of emerging global digital communities. As Airbnb has grown into a global behemoth, Chesky has refocused his energies on 'keep[ing] the community at the centre of what we do'. To achieve this – and to reaffirm the importance of community to Airbnb – Chesky decided 'to change my title from CEO to CEO and Head of Community'.[2]

Radiating confidence and charisma, Chesky is chatting away in the lingo of the start-up world. 'Airbnb started really as a community, probably even more than a business', Chesky recounts. Just your typical Y-Combinator-incubated, Sequoia Capital-funded, Silicon Valley community. He continues, 'it became a business to scale the community. But the point is that when it became a business it never stopped becoming a community.' Despite the doublespeak, Chesky seems to earnestly believe in the inherent goodness of the company and its positive impact on the world. As Chesky goes on, the question of why other communities have not felt the need to transform into global for-profit businesses to continue their growth seems beside the point: 'I think one of the things that makes Airbnb a bit different from other technology companies is that at other technology companies the product is something you can hold in your hand – it's a piece of software. Our product is our community. It's you. It's people.'[3]

To understand this formulation, 'our product is our community', we need to go back to 2012 and see how Airbnb developed its social mission. From 2012 to 2017, Airbnb had a similar 'glow up' to Facebook, which we saw in Chapter 2. Back in 2012, its Twitter bio read: 'Airbnb connects travellers seeking authentic experiences with hosts offering unique, inspiring spaces around the world.' But as we have seen, 'connecting people' is so 2000s. Airbnb soon changed it to 'the world's largest community-driven hospitality company', one which enabled you to #BelongAnywhere.

Belong anywhere – it's both a lovely thought and a slightly ominous premonition of the company's growing omnipresence. For to belong *anywhere* in the very brand-specific way Airbnb management have in mind, Airbnb properties have to exist *everywhere* – in every country, in thousands of cities and in millions of neighbourhoods across the globe. As we will see, the growth of the Airbnb 'community' has often been at the expense of the very communities it claims to serve.

CULTING THE AIRBNB COMMUNITY

The journey began when Chesky got in touch with brand guru Douglas Atkin. 'You know a lot about Branding. Can you help us define ours?', Chesky inquired. Douglas Atkin's own history helps explain how he came to envision a multi-billion dollar corporation as a community-powered grassroots organisation. During the 1990s, Atkin worked at a number of ad agencies and pioneered techniques in community building and brand storytelling that he would take into the tech start-up world. Atkin's book, *The Culting of Brands: Turn Your Customers into True Believers*, studied how and why people join cults in order to gain insight into how companies could foster brand loyalty and commitment.[4] Atkin relates how 'all those lessons that I learnt were applicable to any kind of community, whether you're starting a cult, a religion, a company, whatever'.[5] He moved from the world of marketing to digital community building when he became a partner at MeetUp. He then started a consultancy service called Purpose and helped launch AllOut.org, an online advocacy group for LGBTQ issues.

His journey has allowed him to speak the language of social movements in generic shibboleths that offer a sense of higher purpose to corporations. He relates all of his experience back to the central theme of 'how communities can change the world'. Atkin's twenty-first-century corporate mysticism repackages insights from social movement activists in the language of empowerment and community building. This brand of 'seventies radicalism meets corporate marketing' has found a welcome home with Silicon Valley executives.

Atkin would go on to become global head of community and mobilisation at Airbnb and is credited with playing a key role in developing its mission, values and culture. His response to Chesky's invitation is telling of the direction in which Airbnb would move:

> I think that instead of the Brand, we should figure out the Purpose of Airbnb and its community. There clearly is a huge and vital community of Hosts, Guests and Employees. Let's figure out what role Airbnb plays in their lives and why they are committed to it. If we can do that, then it will be much easier to figure out what Airbnb's Brand is. But not just that. You will be able to decide *everything* more easily: who to recruit, what products to develop, what businesses to buy, what your building should look like. Everything. It's the rudder that guides the ship.[6]

FINDING AIRBNB'S PURPOSE

When Atkin arrived he assembled a team to go door to door listening to hosts and travellers about what Airbnb meant to them. Atkin scribbled down ideas as people spoke to him about discovering their 'inner adventurer', becoming 'insiders' in a new city and feeling like no matter where they went they were 'the World's local'. He was looking for transformative moments that happened when people used Airbnb's service. This, he thought, would provide the key for unlocking its mission.

All of the different stories kept coming back to similar themes, which Atkin distilled into a single purpose for the company: 'Airbnb and its community wants to create a world where Anyone can Belong Anywhere.' As he describes it: 'It was an ambition that was rooted in the everyday experienced truth of its users, but it also stretched into something much bigger, highly desirable, and could have positive impact on the world.'[7]

Airbnb has built its company philosophy around the value of belonging and global community. 'For so long, people thought Airbnb was about renting houses. But really, we're about home', Chesky wrote in

Airbnb Magazine. 'You see, a house is just a space, but a home is where you belong. And what makes this global community so special is that for the very first time, you can belong anywhere.'[8] Airbnb even developed its own symbol, the 'Bélo', the company logo which looks suspiciously similar to Habitat's 'heart home' logo, designed in 2002. In a promotional video introducing the design, Airbnb offers a clear vision of its newly discovered role, facilitating meaningful relationships in an increasingly alienated and disconnected world.[9] The purpose of the company was to create a safer, more open and more tolerant world in which anybody could experience a sense of community and belonging.

It spreads this message by sharing stories of its hosts and other members of the community. If you scroll through its social media accounts or flick through the pages of *Airbnb Magazine*, you will read hundreds of stories of quirky superhosts, unique homes and authentic travel experiences. It's all part of a carefully curated brand storytelling exercise designed to associate the company with experiences of belonging and community.

MICRO-ENTREPRENEURS OF THE WORLD UNITE!

Since 2013, Airbnb has imagined itself not simply as a community but as a grassroots organisation and social movement. This kind of language could be dismissed as empty tech-speak, but it has profoundly shaped how Airbnb engages with the world. Douglas Atkin isn't exaggerating when he says: 'we are doing some pretty new things at Airbnb that haven't been done before at any company'.[10]

Airbnb has raised an army by developing a global corporate-driven social movement of its hosts to confront regulators who stand in its way. It has raided the toolbox of community organising and social movement history to forge new strategies to further its corporate goals.

In the development of the company's philosophy from 2012 to 2014, Airbnb began to be imagined as a fusion of a social movement and grassroots organisation. 'Those are the two formats that do enable communities to scale and take action', explains Atkin, 'mushing them together' is what allows the management team 'to do what we are doing at Airbnb'.[11] According to Atkin's vision, Airbnb grew from a short-term rental matchmaker into a global force for democratisation, economic empowerment and community building.

One of the more innovative aspects of Airbnb's strategy is its combination of lobbying efforts with hosts' grassroots-style organising. In 2015,

Airbnb announced it would 'support the creation of 100 independent Home Sharing Clubs in 100 cities around the world'.[12] Airbnb's Home Sharing Clubs programme was an attempt to foster the development of civic society organisations that would act as 'a powerful people-to-people based political advocacy bloc'.[13] To help form these 'independent' organisations, Airbnb began hiring 'community organisers' who were paid professionals that would embed themselves in local Airbnb communities and encourage hosts to take action. Douglas Atkin called the programme Firestarter. It was an approach to community mobilisation that drew on the 'snowflake' model of the Obama campaign in which paid staff would train community leaders to recruit their own volunteers. New recruits would be given ever larger roles as they moved up the 'commitment curve' and became more involved in the campaign.

The clubs aimed to 'advocate for fair and clear home sharing regulations in their city, share best practices around hosting and hospitality, organize community service activities, and can serve as a forum to connect those who share a passion for home sharing'.[14] We could speak of Airbnb's development of 'micro-lobbyists': organised groups of platform users who mobilise to put pressure on municipal governments and other regulatory bodies. Chris Lehane, head of global policy and communications, announced that 'many of these organizations have already been formed. In other places, we've heard from hosts who want to get involved, but just need a little assistance.' In a job advertisement, Airbnb stated, 'We are looking for a team of Community Organisers to support our hosts' right to homeshare, build close working relationships with community leaders and work with our hosts and guests to find the best ways to be good neighbours.'[15] The company sought out people with 'experience in community organising within political campaigns, the charity or government sectors or grassroots campaigns'.[16] Political experience was seen as desirable, although the precise aims of the clubs were specifically left vague and ambiguous.

Some of the organisers didn't see their jobs in such political terms. As Laura Ward, a London community organiser, where Airbnb has had fewer Home Sharing Clubs, explained, 'it is about getting hosts together so they can learn and help each other. They can share ideas, share problems, and, by coming to these meetings, they have a direct line to Airbnb that can be really helpful. They get to know each other and do not feel they are letting someone come into their home in isolation.'[17]

It's also important to keep in mind that hosts are not passive dupes. Many of these hosts are platform entrepreneurs themselves whose Airbnb business is affected by tighter regulations on the short-term rental market. They are therefore committed to helping Airbnb fight regulators because the company's lobbying efforts and continued legality enables their own profitable enterprise.

How successful has this strategy been in practice? Airbnb put this model to work in 2015 against San Francisco when city regulators introduced Proposition F, which attempted to restrict home rental in the city.[18] Following protests against the effects of Airbnb, the city wanted to receive reports on quarterly data, reduce the total number of days hosts could rent out entire homes and require hosts to register with the city.

Airbnb spent US$8 million on a campaign against the city which included TV ads, a door-to-door field campaign and snarky billboards which read 'Dear Public Library System, we hope you use some of the US$12 million in hotel taxes to keep the library open later. Love, Airbnb.' But for Atkin, 'mobilisation was absolutely instrumental in changing the law ... we got about 250 of our hosts to show up at land use hearings and to give up a day of work'.[19] Airbnb had mobilised hosts in defence of the platform and successfully defeated the city's attempt to apply moderate regulations on their business. 'We basically drenched lawmakers with our community,' Atkin gloated, 'we totally overwhelmed them.' Airbnb 'hired many of the people who did the grassroots campaigning for Obama in 2008 and 2012' and put them through an 'Obama-style training' to turn them into 'machines delivering the soft skill of relationship building and community building'.[20]

Atkin believed that 'overwhelming' publicly elected lawmakers had produced a win for democracy because Airbnb positions itself as a true representative of the people. Airbnb is framed as a 'people-to-people platform' embodying the very principles of democracy properly understood: 'we are of the people, by the people and for the people'.[21] It's as if by rhetorical magic alone, one can trace a direct lineage from Lincoln's Gettysburg address to Atkin's latest TED talk.

In truth, the platform enables the company to mobilise a very particular subsection of the people – those who can transform urban housing into spaces of domestic entrepreneurialism. Airbnb has created and expanded a new market in short-term rentals outside of the hotel industry, which has not only disrupted tourism and hospitality but has created a new political struggle between groups of 'Airbnb Citizens' and municipal and city councils.

CORPORATE COMMUNITY ORGANISING

In many respects, the tradition of community organising presents an ideal resource for the company because intransigent local councils have typically been the target of community organisers.[22] It also points to a malleability of the tradition. The pragmatic and non-ideological approach of community organisers leaves the tradition without an over-arching vision of an ideal society. The framework encourages building people power and focusing on 'immediate, specific, and winnable issues' for the purpose of growing the organisation and building the collective power of its members.[23] The difference is that in traditional community organising it is 'people versus power' rather than the powerful using people as a tool to achieve their policy objectives.

When Obama's campaign team adopted certain aspects of the rhetoric and tactics of community organising for his election campaigns in 2008 and 2012 they did so only by creating a fundamental contradiction: were communities organising for their own power or to get Obama elected?[24] The two objectives weren't mutually exclusive, but in the heat of an election campaign the temptation is always to prioritise voter identification and turnout. There is something deeply antithetical to the spirit of community organising in mobilising citizens for the instrumental goal of electing a politician or securing a policy victory for a company.

With Airbnb, the appropriation of certain ideas and techniques from community organising comes with dubious consequences for genuine community empowerment. It's accompanied by rhetorical moves that abstract from the history, material reality and social positions of the struggle between the 'hayes' and the 'have nots'. Atkin is interested in 'how movements get huge numbers of people to take the same action and make a huge difference in the world'. But the constitution of the people, the nature of the actions and the quality of the difference are all left open, with people encouraged to fill in the gaps with sepia-toned images from the civil rights era. In Atkin's model of social change, the increase in the power, resilience and self-confidence of a community is left by the wayside. It is enough for Airbnb's entrepreneurial hosts to operate their businesses in a slightly less regulated environment.

More recently, Airbnb has continued to promote the mythology of its hosts as consisting primarily of 'mom-and-pop' outfits helping create magical and unique moments for their guests.[25] Its advertising campaign of early 2021, 'Made Possible by Hosts', consists of a series of short films showcasing Airbnb homes from different locations around the world. 'We basically say we're a community of entrepreneurs or micro-entrepreneurs', Chesky noted.[26] The term 'micro-entrepreneur' seems to have been invented because if hosts truly were entrepreneurs it would involve growing into multi-property investors. The reality of Airbnb today is that the majority of hosts do in fact have multiple listings and are run by professional rental companies. From August 2017 to September 2020 hosts with one property have shrunk from 47 per cent to just 37 per cent of all listings.[27] During this same period hosts with between 101 and 1,000 properties increased by 50 per cent. In September 2020, 14 per cent of hosts had more than 21 listings on the platform.

This reflects the changing nature of Airbnb and the short-term rental industry, which is shifting from a 'person-to-person' model of individual hosts on one platform to a 'business-to-consumer' model of property management companies with multiple listings on multiple platforms simultaneously. Many of these companies such as Sonder and Vacasa seek to build their own platforms and establish direct relationships with consumers, sometimes through their own software and systems. The problem with this emerging reality is that the idea of professional managers doesn't fit so well with Airbnb's self-portrait of a company that only wishes to help middle-class families rent out their spare rooms.

COMMUNITY-WASHING AS BRAND STRATEGY

The constant appeals to the notion of an Airbnb community are designed to hide the negative social consequences of their business model behind a feel-good veneer of community building. We could call this 'community-washing' – the corporate marketing strategy of framing the activities of the company in the language of community empowerment and fulfilling a social mission. The aim is to drown out questions of substantial user fees, tax avoidance, venture capital funding and the company's litigious history with stories of interesting hosts and travel experiences.

By blurring the lines between community and company, Airbnb is engaged in an insincere gesture to pass itself off as a social enterprise. According to the spin of tech CEOs, making billions of dollars is almost incidental to – or a welcome but unexpected by-product of – their social mission of connecting the world and giving people a sense of belonging in community. But we have reason to be suspicious of these claims from the world's leading 'community-washers' like Facebook and Airbnb because in nearly every single case the business came first and the sense of purpose was invented along the way. It was a post hoc rationalisation of the company's purpose that sought to provide a more polished and idealised explanation of its business activities. The social mission of these companies was developed years after the company's founding and usually as a direct result of PR issues and pressure from the public.

It's important to remember that the most prominent tech founders were not working at charities, non-governmental organisations or philanthropic organisations when they stumbled upon their ideas. They were not trying to meaningfully counteract power hierarchies or redress growing social and economic inequalities. They were students, software engineers and industrial designers who were all trying to develop new products. Typically, these young, privileged American men were looking to start a business and get rich. What they all had in common was less a shared passion for community and more a drive to monetise their ideas and build an empire.

The strategy of community-washing serves a number of important goals for the company. First, the language of community triggers what cognitive linguist George Lakoff calls a 'frame': a set of associated images and concepts that can be positively linked to the brand.[28] The idea of an Airbnb community can be used to attract new customers by aligning the platform with positive social values, giving users a sense of contributing to a larger social mission. When you stay at an Airbnb house, the company claims, you're not just booking short-term accommodation, you're contributing to a global movement of community building. With every trip you're fighting prejudice and tearing down the walls of social alienation.

The language also helps Airbnb attract the best talent to work for the company. Three in four millennials consider a company's social and environmental commitments before deciding where to work. They want to be part of something bigger and work for a company with a social purpose. As Airbnb itself recognises, 'a positive contribution to society' is increasingly 'what citizens, consumers, employees, communities, and policy-makers desire – even demand'.[29] The wager is that by embracing the discourse of corporate social responsibility businesses can ultimately benefit their bottom line through increased user engagement and employee satisfaction.

The frame of community is also an important defensive manoeuvre because it evokes ideas of tolerance, forgiveness and working together to solve common problems. The strategy locates the company in a space of positive outlook and good intentions. As part of 'the community', Airbnb is able to talk about itself as forever in the process of 'working on issues', 'trying really hard' and 'acknowledging its mistakes'. When issues do arise, the answer is never external regulation or restrictions on the company. This attitude of 'always accountable, but always failing' enables companies to gain positive news stories from launching initiatives to solve problems of their own creation.

Community-washing allows companies to position themselves as self-designated leaders of communities with the epistemic authority to speak on their behalf and address their issues. This has the perverse result that Airbnb sees itself as best placed to solve issues caused by its own actions. It's seen as a matter for the management to have a big think and come up with a solution that's right for their community. 'Oftentimes we sit in a room trying to make decisions,' Chesky recounts, 'and of course we are from the community – but I want to make sure that when we're making a decision for the community we are doing it *for* the community not *to* the community'.[30] The correct phrase, even for relatively mainstream development work, is *with* the community, not for it. Whether its 'for' or 'to', it's still a unilateral action of one party on another.

But numerous issues such as discrimination on the platform, housing unaffordability and the destruction of the character of local communities have only been addressed in a reactive manner when they make headlines and threaten the reputation of the company. In 2018 – ten years after Airbnb's launch – Chesky announced his intention to publish a Stakeholder Report and could say with a straight face, 'this is Day One for us'. He continued, 'And I hope more and more companies follow the lead, rather than just cherry-picking certain issues. Just think very broadly about the impact you have on the world'.[31] Just think about it guys, really.

AIRBNB'S UNDERCOVER WAR ON COMMUNITIES

Behind the marketing material, there's a growing disconnect between the glossy image of itself that Airbnb presents in its social media output and the realities of how the business is affecting communities. The story of mutual benefit and limited costs has become increasingly difficult to sustain as Airbnb has continued to expand, with a growing collection of scientific studies and news reports casting doubt over its noble intentions and positive impact on local communities. The reality is that when it comes to real-world communities – and not just those that appear in Airbnb's marketing material – the company has often fought hard to protect its own interests and profitability over the health and well-being of citizens.

Analysis conducted by the Economic Policy Institute, a non-partisan American think tank, reported that the economic costs of Airbnb to local communities likely outweighed the benefits.[32] Research from the *Harvard Business Review* found that Airbnb is negatively affecting the housing stock across the US due to the incentive for landlords to take properties out of the long-term rental market and turn them into profitable short-term rentals.[33] A report from the *Guardian* in early 2020 also found that Airbnb is threatening affordable housing across the UK.[34] Airbnb rentals have become so prevalent in some parts of the country that there is up to one listing for every four properties, prompting calls for increased government regulation and for a 90-day cap on all homes let on the platform.

Despite the many public statements by Airbnb executives about partnering with cities and working with local communities, Airbnb has been one of the most litigious start-ups in Silicon Valley, fighting cities across the world in an attempt to avoid regulations. Since launching in 2008, Airbnb has been involved in at least eleven lawsuits against local and state authorities in America, with legal action taken against Boston, Palm Beach County, Miami Beach and New York.[35] It has used its deep pockets in a protracted campaign to undermine regulators across the US. Officials in Palm Beach County, Florida have been attempting to force Airbnb to collect and pay the county's 6 per cent occupancy tax on visits since 2014. Three lawsuits later and millions of unpaid taxes still remain outstanding. 'We knew we were going to get sued,' Palm Beach County tax collector Anne Gannon reported to *Wired* in 2019, 'that's what they do all over the country. It's their mode of operation.'[36]

In a joint letter written in 2018, Amsterdam, Barcelona, Berlin, Bordeaux, Brussels, Krakow, Munich, Paris, Valencia and Vienna pleaded for the EU to more effectively regulate holiday rental websites like Airbnb, claiming they were reducing the stock of long-term housing and adversely affecting neighbourhoods.[37] Airbnb has ramped up its lobbying efforts in relation to EU institutions, spending millions in efforts to achieve less onerous regulations according to a Corporate Europe Observatory report.

One of the primary threats to Airbnb's business model is enforceable caps on property rentals. Cities such as Amsterdam, London, Paris, Tokyo and San Francisco all have caps of between 60 and 120 days a year. Fears of the success of such a move have prompted Airbnb to demand 'a single European oversight body for digital services', which it could lobby instead of fighting battles against multiple cities.[38]

Throughout its ten-year history, Airbnb has preferred to act without gaining permission and to allow regulators to chase them over violations. The resulting disputes have been like a global game of whack-a-mole, with Airbnb challenging local authorities' attempts to stand up to them. The company fights every battle out of the fear that a particularly onerous set of regulations might prove successful in one city and spark a domino effect across the globe.

Lawmakers who do not introduce Airbnb-friendly legislation are seen as obstacles that need to be overcome. For those who disagree, Airbnb's strategy has involved 'using people power to demonstrate this is a good thing for cities and a good thing for citizens'. The company agitates against what it sees as repressive local regulators that are 'in the pockets' of rival businesses and 'the hotel lobby'. 'The sharing economy is new,' states Douglas Atkin, 'but the laws are old and we are bumping up against old laws and old incumbents.'[39]

What is clear in this pattern of behaviour is that Airbnb's priority every step of the way has been to ensure that stricter regulations do not affect its future business opportunities. Concerns about Airbnb's negative impact on communities have only worried them following negative press, with the whole endeavour treated primarily as a PR exercise. Airbnb is prepared to work with cities so long as its business interests are not adversely affected. But in many cases, the rhetoric has simply been a smokescreen for a company that originally preferred to operate with as minimal regulations as possible.

Airbnb has consistently put its corporate interests ahead of those of local communities. In instances where being responsible and abiding by a city's regulations has threatened its profitability, it has fought tooth and nail to undermine and defeat local elected representatives. Its fight against San Francisco, which was eventually settled out of court, cost the city about US$330,000 in legal fees.[40]

Airbnb's behaviour has also opened up a new industry of companies offering assistance to local authorities attempting to regulate short-stay accommodation. The company's reluctance to release its data to local authorities has led to the creation of organisations such as AirDNA and Inside Airbnb, the latter being 'an independent, non-commercial set of tools and data that allows you to explore how Airbnb is being used in cities around the world', administered by community activist Murray Cox.[41] Since Airbnb rarely releases data of its operations, it's difficult to have an informed public debate over their policies and their effect on cities.

AIRBNB'S REGULATORY ENTREPRENEURSHIP

Its frequent clashes with local and state laws highlight how critical settling legal disputes over laws are to its business. Before their public listing, Airbnb needed to reassure investors that a particularly onerous set of regulations in one city wouldn't prove popular and effective, setting off calls to replicate this across the globe. Airbnb's lobbying and micro-lobbying campaigns are part of a concerted effort to get the regulations it needs to support its business.

Legal scholars Elizabeth Pollman and Jordan M. Barry have called this activity 'regulatory entrepreneurship', which they define as 'pursuing a line of business in which changing the law is a significant part of the business plan'.[42] This is not new, but it has become more relevant now with tech companies such as Airbnb and Uber who are well funded, scalable and target state and local laws through high-profile legal and political contests. It's not simply about lobbying. It involves a company's core business activities operating in a murky zone of possible illegality, making working towards a change in the regulatory framework an integral aspect of its business model.

Regulatory entrepreneurs, the scholars argue, employ a host of new tactics to achieve their commercial and political goals:

> The conventional story of corporate political power relies on gaining quiet access to officials, then leveraging that access to exert influence behind the scenes. While regulatory entrepreneurs have sometimes used these tried-and-true methods, they have become better known, and arguably have experienced greater success, from the opposite

strategy: they make an issue as publicly salient as possible, rally the public to their cause, then use their popular support as leverage to win the change they want from resistant officials.[43]

Airbnb has had its fair share of public campaigns against laws from San Francisco and New York, to Barcelona and Paris. But there has been a more recent shift in Airbnb's strategy and the tone of its PR campaign on this issue. As the company has grown, it has toned down its mean-spirited billboards and talk of itself as a plucky upstart looking to disrupt the hotel industry. Airbnb increasingly sees itself as a long-term key player in global tourism and wants to have a seat at the table in its governance.

The Home Sharing Clubs are part of a broader PR campaign called Airbnb Citizen, inaugurated in November 2016, which publishes reports, tells branded stories and places Airbnb as a 'thought leader' in the industry. Sponsoring corporate-driven community organising has been just one of the ways Airbnb has sought to 'advance home sharing as a solution'. Airbnb Citizen 'promotes home sharing's potential to help solve many of the economic, environmental and social challenges we face today'.[44] It's designed to represent the Airbnb 'movement' and to act as a hub for their organisers, volunteer micro-lobbyists and other hosts.

As part of their campaign to set the agenda for policy- and law-making, Airbnb has published a 'Policy Tool Chest' which assists governments in designing home-share-friendly regulations. In this document and elsewhere, Airbnb put forward recommendations with respect to data sharing, neighbourhood safety, tourist taxes and other policy challenges. The idea behind the document is to offer a kit of flexible tools that can be quickly adapted to different political settings across the globe.

In September 2020, the company also launched 'Airbnb City Portal', a 'first-of-its-kind resource for governments' aimed at reducing efforts in establishing partnerships with cities.[45] It offers cities data and tools for creating regulations that are beneficial for the company. This partnership activity is an attempt to build institutional legitimacy and to cast regulation as a collaborative exercise that should involve companies in the process.

Airbnb has increasingly emphasised its role as a partner in co-operative models of urban governance, depicting itself as a dependable partner and reliable member of the community. In mid-2020, the opening video on the Airbnb Citizen YouTube page was entitled 'Supporting Communities', which showcased this new tone in their public relations campaign:

At Airbnb we know that protecting the places we love takes better regulations. It's why we support thriving communities by collecting and submitting taxes from our guests. Its why we support host registration requirements for safer neighbourhoods. And its why we're helping to preserve neighbourhoods by providing reporting tools to neighbours to hold us accountable.[46]

Airbnb has good reason to see itself as an important voice in the global tourism industry. It is ubiquitous across nearly every country on the planet and its use has dramatically altered urban geographies. Its popularity and growth raise troubling questions about the role it plays as infrastructure relied upon by the general public. We return to this issue in Chapter 7 in our discussion of the increasingly public role of platforms in our societies.

THE RETURN OF A STAKEHOLDER SOCIETY

'We're gonna need to consider our impact on society', Chesky declared in 2018 after a decade of running a global business that affected millions of people; 'what I've basically been saying is most companies are oriented around a 20th century model. It's a little bit more short term. You serve your shareholders. And I think society expects more of us.'[47] Airbnb had long been talking about 'strengthening the neighborhoods and cities we serve' and building 'strong partnerships with cities all over the globe'.[48] But the concept of 'stakeholder theory' offered a new framework to recast the firm's purpose and its relationship to society. It was the final step that cemented existing strategies from its 2015 'Community Compact' to Airbnb Citizen and Home Sharing Clubs. Airbnb publically declared that the company was not simply shareholder-driven but would attempt to serve all of its stakeholders, including guests, hosts, employees, communities and shareholders.

In the US and UK, the rights of shareholders are considered sacrosanct and have been enshrined in law as a legal obligation for company directors to protect. Neoliberal economist Milton Friedman's famous view was that 'there is one and only one social responsibility of business – to use its resources to engage in activities designed to increase its profits'.[49] Stakeholder theory considers the proper role of a firm as one that actively contributes to the betterment of society and pursues shareholder value as one among multiple other social goods.

It experienced its first surge in popularity in the 1990s, partly in response to the perceived excesses of 1980s finance capitalism. In the UK, New Labour were searching for their 'big idea' that could act as a unifying vision around which other policy proposals could be organised. Will Hutton's book, *The State We're In*, offered the concept of 'stakeholder capitalism' as an alternative to the short-termist free market ideology of the 1980s.[50] On 8 January 1996, at a keynote speech to business groups in Singapore, the Labour Party leader, Tony Blair, set out his vision of a 'stakeholder economy' as one 'in which opportunity is available to all, advancement is through merit, and from which no group or class is set apart or excluded'.[51] The central idea was about the role of trust between employers, employees and government and the 'recognition of mutual purpose'. Like Chesky, Blair also spoke of the need to move towards a 'twenty-first century' model of economic thinking and embrace the 'limitless potential' of new technologies.

The idea was adopted in Labour's 1997 manifesto, which called for a 'stakeholder economy ... where everyone has a stake in society and owes responsibilities to it'.[52] The model spoke to New Labour's interest in reforming welfare and in widening social participation. It could support a broad agenda of reformist capitalism without getting too specific about what needed to change.

Stakeholder theory appealed to a range of centre-left economists and political actors during the 1990s. One of the benefits of the idea was that it sounded like a variety of appealing things to different people across the political spectrum. As cabinet minister William Waldegrave noted in the Commons, 'to the floating voter, it can be made to sound like the good old Conservative idea of the property-owning democracy ... wider ownership of homes, shares and pension funds. There is nothing threatening in that, which is why the phrase was used'.[53] To a leftist, it can evoke images of a fundamental restructure of capitalist firms and the economy. Incorporating stakeholders could mean a push for pluralist forms of ownership and management to benefit workers, communities and the environment. The vagueness and openness of the term helps explain its appeal as an idea with a promising sounding ring but potentially few practical implications to hold those in power accountable.

A NEW CORPORATE PURPOSE

In 2019, the idea was back on the global agenda after the Business Roundtable announced the release of a new Statement on the Purpose of a Corporation.[54] This declaration was signed by 181 CEOs who committed to lead their companies for the benefit of all stakeholders – customers, employees, suppliers, communities and shareholders. The statement affirmed that corporate responsibilities extend beyond shareholders and that corporations should embed social impact in their corporate purpose. This was a remarkable document from a group who had periodically released Principles of Corporate Governance, which since 1978 had all reflected the centrality of shareholder primacy. The statement released in August 2019, read:

> We believe the free-market system is the best means of generating good jobs, a strong and sustainable economy, innovation, a healthy environment and economic opportunity for all. … While each of our individual companies serves its own corporate purpose, we share a fundamental commitment to all of our stakeholders.[55]

The statement was widely celebrated by top CEOs, who saw it as a welcome call for firms to 'invest in their employees and communities', and as a 'promising way to build long-term value', in the words of Tricia Griffith, president and CEO of Progressive Corporation.[56] This became a central theme of the World Economic Forum's fiftieth meeting in 2020 under the title: 'Stakeholders for a Cohesive and Sustainable World'. According to the 2020 Davos Manifesto, it was the responsibility of a company 'to understand and harmonize the divergent interests of all stakeholders' to improve opportunities for long-term prosperity.[57] This was the first time the manifesto had been updated in over 40 years, proclaiming a company's purpose 'to engage all its stakeholders in shared and sustained value creation'.

If shareholder capitalism was so unfit for purpose, why had it been allowed to dominate for decades? And why was it only the purpose of the company that had to change as a result? By locating the necessary changes that needed to occur at the level of the firm, were they not putting themselves in charge of how to rein in – themselves? But what if such a voluntary pledge of self-abnegation was simply a mechanism to ward off calls for more far-reaching structural reform? Pitching stakeholder capitalism as 'the best opportunity to tackle today's environmental and social challenges' has to be seen against the backdrop of the Sanders/Warren insurgency within the Democratic Party and the rise of socialist movements across the globe. As we will see, taking the interests of a vaguely defined collection of stakeholders into account can be easily achieved by a series of tokenistic efforts.

Two years after their initial announcement Airbnb reported that they were still 'early in our work'. In January 2020, a 1,500-word document was released, with a soon to be broken promise to publish a first Annual Stakeholder Report in March that year.[58] At the time of writing no such report has been published, and all we are left with are some general indications and a list of possible metrics for verifying progress. The timing of the 'update' also raised suspicions that its release was oriented more towards a box-ticking exercise before their initial public offering (IPO) rather than a genuine engagement with the issue.

A TRUST EXERCISE

The tech world asks us to trust them. They reassure us that they want to be held accountable. But this requires us to believe in the disinterested benevolence of the powerful and that a fair balance between competing interests can be satisfactorily achieved by one of the parties to the case. No coherent moral philosophy has ever considered this possible. This is even more so for corporations where there is a tendency for those within the firm to trust in their own good intentions and see no problem in taking over the decision-making of others.

The fundamental flaw is that corporations don't see themselves as a threat. The idea of balancing interests will always be weighted in favour of the corporation because the underlying presumption is that it's the corporation that creates wealth, jobs and social value. From this perspective, the negative externalities produced by profit maximisation can never be adequately addressed.

When community building and mechanisms of accountability are treated as a design challenge for the powerful, they fail to adequately serve the interests of those they purport to represent. The problem with the current process is that there is no real change to the balance of economic power. Those in power concede nothing and have merely set up a new regime for administering the demands of those affected by their behaviour. The stakeholder model provides the façade of ethical practice while giving up no real power and setting the terms upon which any future stakeholder engagement will take place. It also allows Airbnb to generate positive news stories with big promises whose results will not be seen for a number of years.

Airbnb has bounced back quicker than expected from the pandemic, and finished 2020 with a spectacularly successful public listing in which their share price doubled on the first day of trading, valuing the company at over US$100 billion.[59] The company began seeing signs of recovery as early as June 2020, with only a slight drop in their bookings from the same month in 2019. With the company now launched on the stock market, it is clear which of their 'communities' will take priority in the months ahead.

4

Private Power and Public Infrastructure

What do you do when something you rely on every day breaks down? For some people, you call the police. 'Yes, our @YouTube is down, too. No, please don't call 911 – we can't fix it', tweeted Philadelphia Police late in the evening on 17 October 2018.[1] For almost two hours, YouTube experienced a rare outage, and people just didn't know what to do. The video-sharing platform was inaccessible and either showed a server error message, a blank page or broken images when people attempted to access the website. Twitter was quick to mock those who turned to their local law enforcement agency in the hope of having their cat videos returned. But the incident highlights the increasingly blurred lines in people's conception of public and private providers of services.

Global platforms like Facebook and Google now occupy an ambiguous position: they are widely accessible services used by many as if they were public utilities but which are run as for-profit companies. Control over how these services are designed and operated gives digital platforms enormous power to shape the digital public sphere. They influence what information and news is available to us, how we communicate with others and the limits of political debate. Thankfully, many have begun to wake up to the threat these services pose to the proper functioning of our democracies and to the very existence of an independent civil society. Whether we like it or not, the ranking and ordering algorithms of digital platforms now provide essential infrastructure of our public sphere, giving private companies significant power to shape its content and character.[2]

The question of who owns and controls digital infrastructure is not a problem with a purely technical solution. It is a political issue that concerns the distribution of power in society and which institutional arrangements will keep this in check. Algorithms will necessarily privilege one group's interests over another and require important decisions about competing values and principles of how to regulate public speech. How major platforms design their algorithms and the operation of their platforms actually consists in a de facto public policy-making. As a result, private control over digital infrastructure enables companies to shape the structural conditions of our politics.

We need to push for social ownership and democratic control of platforms like Google, Facebook and Twitter so we can have a greater say in how they operate. Organisations that operate this digital infrastructure should be accountable to the public interest. Nationalising and remunicipalising public utilities is common sense in many places around the world and can lead to more efficient and better-run services.[3] Open and inclusive platforms provide mechanisms for people to participate in them and decide on how they are organised. Instituting different forms of social ownership is not a panacea to all our problems, but it does allow us to assert our collective democratic power against the private rule of economic elites.

Before we turn to this, it is worth examining other approaches to tackling the many problems of Big Tech. Current debates about technology take place on terrain that is favourable to the platform giants. Critics tend to treat the symptoms rather than the causes and propose insufficiently robust measures to counter the problems they diagnose. Most existing ideas for reform are limited by their individualist, market-driven and consumer-oriented framing of the issues. Our political imagination has been so restricted that even our wildest dreams of taking back control are enmeshed in the same Silicon Valley logic that caused the problems in the first place.

NO NEW DEAL ON DATA

Our first concern with tech companies is often Big Brother issues about surveillance, privacy and data breaches. For example, 85 per cent of Americans are concerned about the amount of data online platforms store about them and whether they are selling this information to third parties without their knowledge.[4] Tech giants should face tighter regulations on their handling of data, but this wouldn't necessarily disrupt their power or impede their current business models. Personal data was always the means not the end. So long as ownership and control over the platform itself is not affected, companies can find ways to work around constraints like the European Union's General Data Protection Regulation, which tend to hit smaller competitors harder, further extending the big players' market dominance because they are the most capable of complying with the regulations.[5] A focus on data breaches such as the Cambridge Analytica scandal also normalises the exploitative practices of the companies by assuming that there is a 'safe' and acceptable standard they could strive for within their current model.

Not everyone is happy with the current practices of Big Tech owning our personal data. Former American presidential candidate, Andrew Yang, has been among the most prominent supporters of what is known as a data dividend.[6] This proposal has gained ground as a 'New Deal on Data', which was defined by MIT professor Sandy Petland as 'a rebalancing of the ownership of data in favor of the individual whose data is collected. People would have the same rights they now have over their physical bodies and their money.'[7]

The problem with this approach is that it risks further entrenching the existing model while simultaneously making it even more difficult to introduce an alternative. Considered from Yang's consumer-oriented perspective, there is also the troubling question of global inequalities in the value of different people's data. In the third quarter of 2020, Facebook's average revenue per user in the Asia-Pacific region was US$3.67, compared with US$39.63 in the combined US and Canada market.[8] There is a tension between the language of data ownership as a 'human right' and the commercial fact that advertisers pay more for access to different markets. Are we comfortable with a framework in which some people's market-mediated human rights could be worth ten times more than others?

More important, however, are the political shortcomings of the movement. The data dividend proposal does not contest corporations' right to harvest and use individuals' data. If data becomes a new source of revenue for citizens it extends a model of the capitalisation of our everyday lives even deeper into society, raising new concerns about how the financial worth of every aspect of our online interactions might be maximised. It doesn't grapple with the potentially horrific consequences of a world in which every thought and emotion would be partially oriented towards potential buyers on a data market. The beginning of this turn towards monetising our personalities and lifestyles has already begun, but it should not be further cemented through such a scheme. This would create more barriers for commons-based alternatives, which could not afford to pay data dividends because they don't intend to extract as much profit from their users.

This consumer-oriented response fails to consider the intractable political nature of the problem. Even if the movement was to gain momentum, the entrenched power and deep pockets of the companies would enable them to negotiate the terms of a data dividend to be as favourable to them as possible. It may even increase the power of tech companies by giving them more loyal followers who are paid for their services. Instead of focusing exclusively on the consumer–company relationship, questions of citizenship and democracy need to enter the picture. Platforms serve a public purpose and exploit users as a group. We need solutions framed in terms of collective solidarity not personal rights.

BIG TECH IS NOT AFRAID OF A BOYCOTT

Another group of critics are concerned with the growing size and power of tech companies and propose a range of reforms to rein them in. The first line of attack has been calls for better self-regulation of the sector and the need for these companies to 'develop a conscience'. This is the preferred option for most companies as it allows them to appoint their own internal bodies to help the company 'do better' and hold themselves accountable to the public through intermittent PR campaigns. There are obvious limitations to placing a company whose motto used to be 'move fast and break things' in charge of their own meticulous self-regulation. Even Mark Zuckerberg himself has called for a 'more active role for governments and regulators'.[9] After a decade of wilful blindness to the negative consequences of their business practices, the idea of tech companies deciding to regulate themselves should be a non-starter.

Another possibility is either user or advertiser boycotts. The problem with the former is that users don't usually pay platforms such as Google and Facebook any money, making their displeasure a reputational rather than an economic concern for the companies. Previous user boycott campaigns have gone absolutely nowhere. One prominent 24-hour boycott of Facebook in 2018 coincided with Zuckerberg's appearance before US Congress.[10] Although it achieved significant publicity, its vague demand that Facebook improve its protection of user privacy had little practical effect. A platform as big as Facebook is used to the occasional revolt and nothing has been able to dent its continual growth in users since 2004.

Tech companies have also faced waves of advertiser boycotts, usually triggered by content moderation issues and concerns of brands appearing alongside inappropriate content. In June 2020, a campaign was launched to pressure advertisers to pull ads from Facebook until they changed their moderation practices relating to hateful and racist content.[11] The movement attracted a number of prominent brands, many of whom signed up to a one-month boycott in July 2020. Facebook's stock dropped 8 per cent in a single day, but Zuckerberg believed the company could weather the storm without changing any of its practices.

He was right. Profits for Facebook's largely ad-based business still rose during that financial quarter to US$18.7 billion.[12] Of Facebook's US$70 billion advertising revenue, the ads pulled were a tiny drop in the ocean – the 100 highest-spending brands account for only 6 per cent of the platform's ad revenue.[13] Many of these advertisers were already looking to pull back as a result of Covid-19 and this just gave them an opportunity to make it look like they were taking a stand. As the advertisers had no coherent strategy and no clear demands aside from Facebook 'doing better' on hate speech, it's hard to dispute Zuckerberg's prediction that the advertisers would be 'back on the platform soon enough'.[14]

BREAKING UP BIG TECH IS NOT ENOUGH

A tougher set of opponents have raised issues over how much power big platforms currently exercise over politics, the economy and society. In the economic field, it is claimed that the virtual monopolies of Amazon, Google and Facebook have resulted in an uneven playing field, which has stifled competition and prevented further innovation. The once disruptive and dynamic start-ups have grown into powerful monopolies able to use their resources to lobby regulators and implement laws to suit their own needs. Most notably, Facebook co-founder Chris Hughes has warned of Facebook's growing dominance and called for it to be broken up.[15] Chief among the critics in the political class was Elizabeth Warren during her 2020 presidential campaign.

While the diagnosis was on point – many of these companies clearly *do* exercise too much power in society – the proposed solutions fell short of the structural change that is needed. Even if such conglomerates could be broken up into their individual companies they would still be giant privately owned for-profit platforms with billions of users run primarily for the benefit of the company's shareholders. This also raises questions of how a company like Google or Facebook could be broken up in a meaningful way. It doesn't make sense for every country or region to have their own search engine and walled social network. The global spread of these services is precisely what makes them socially useful. The public would not benefit if Facebook were broken up into three dozen separate companies that competed with one another, as occurred with Standard Oil in 1911.[16] It's also unclear whether Facebook could be prevented from simply merging the digital architecture and systems of a company like Instagram within the Facebook ecosystem in anticipation of antitrust action so that they would no longer exist as two separate companies that could be unmerged.[17]

In both the UK and US, the power and dominance of Big Tech is framed as a problem of unfair competition rather than an extractive and exploitative business model that is in need of reform. Behind the tough-sounding slogan of 'breaking up big tech' lay the much weaker idea of 'restoring competition in the tech sector' by preventing Amazon and others from selling their own products on their transaction platforms.[18] In October 2020, the Judiciary Committee in the US House of Representatives released a damning report following extensive investigation into online platforms and their anticompetitive business practices.[19] The report concluded that 'they not only wield tremendous power, but they also abuse it by charging exorbitant fees, imposing oppressive contract terms, and extracting valuable data from the people and businesses that rely on them'.[20] The underlying concern was to implement stronger antitrust legislation while also undoing several of the Big Tech mergers such as Facebook's purchase of Instagram and WhatsApp. The Biden administration sought to act on these concerns with an executive order in July 2021 which called on US agencies to implement 72 specific provisions, including a mandate to require 'greater scrutiny of mergers, especially by dominant internet platforms'.[21] In the UK, the newly formed Digital Markets Unit of the UK government has been given the power to designate certain tech firms with 'Strategic Market Status' and require them to follow new rules of acceptable behaviour with competitors and customers.[22] The limitations of these competition-focused policies is that they don't challenge the fundamental 'surveillance and commodification' model of the tech sector. There is little that would stop new, smaller competitors from using the same strategies and business models as the current dominant players.

Despite its limitations, Elizabeth Warren's campaign made the important move of framing the biggest platform companies as 'platform utilities'. This idea articulates an understanding of the companies as providing a public service that requires a new model of regulation and control.[23] Individual action and attempts to hold platforms accountable through government oversight provide only piecemeal efforts to disrupt their power. We need a fundamental reorientation of the ownership and governance structures of platforms so they are run for the people and not for profit.

THE CASE FOR DIGITAL PLATFORMS
AS PUBLICLY OWNED UTILITIES

We are accustomed to the idea of power, transport and telecommunications infrastructure as public utilities. These are all essential services provided to the public that would significantly affect their daily lives if they were suspended. The growing size and power of digital platforms has led to calls for the platform giants to be converted into public utilities.[24] Platforms provide access to software and apps that can be distinguished from internet infrastructure – the physical hardware and assemblage of data centres, undersea cables, internet exchange points and national and regional networks that form the backbone of the internet. To extend the idea of public utilities to digital platforms would require stretching the concept beyond the idea of brick-and-mortar infrastructure to a less physical and tangible service. What grounds are there for us to make this leap?

The first argument is that certain digital platforms provide a public service that many people consider essential to their daily lives. Do you need Facebook in the same way you need water? Of course not. But platforms are now widely recognised as necessary services to live a full and rich life in a digital and interconnected world. With each passing year, the argument 'just don't use them' makes less and less sense. The Covid-19 pandemic underscored the critical importance of this digital infrastructure for basic goods and our connection with friends and family. We need to update our understanding of basic services to keep pace with the transformation of social life.

Second, digital platforms are businesses that compete in marketplaces with tendencies towards natural monopolies. This is not the same as the physical infrastructure of railway lines or telephone cables, but the outcomes can be similar: Google has 92.26 per cent of the search market share compared to Bing's 2.83 per cent, while Facebook has 2.85 billion active monthly users compared to Snapchat's 360 million.[25] As we have seen, the operation of network effects leads to advantages accruing to the biggest players. Companies like Facebook and Google have demonstrated the dangers of predatory monopolistic behaviour under such conditions. They provide a service to the public that is difficult for them to turn down and hard to obtain in the same way from other sources. This dependency creates a vulnerability to abuse which tech companies can exploit due to their size and power.

The case for certain digital platforms as public utilities does not rest solely on whether they could be considered natural monopolies. Progressive American reformers of the early twentieth century considered that a much broader range of corporations could justify public regulation and potentially public ownership if their activities were 'affected with a public interest'.[26] This principle was articulated by the Supreme Court in an 1877 case, *Munn* v. *Illinois* in which the court argued that businesses which stored large quantities of grain could be considered a legitimate object of regulation.[27] In cases where the concentration of private power could significantly impact upon the common good, democratic governments had a right to assert public control over their activities. Legal scholar William Novak has shown that 'the legal concept of public utility was capable of justifying state economic controls ranging from statutory police regulation to administrative rate setting to outright public ownership of the means of production'.[28]

While a number of American legal scholars today have argued for the revitalisation of new *regulatory* powers for the US government over digital platforms, platform socialism would seek to go further in addressing questions of *ownership* and *governance* which affect how platforms operate.[29] The limitation of state regulation is that this need not imply greater social empowerment for citizens in how the service is delivered. Public utility regulation adopts a top-down approach of establishing boundaries within which the business can operate and some baselines for service delivery, but this does not entail more wide-reaching changes in terms of workplace democracy and citizen participation. It also sets a narrow horizon on who should exercise greater decision-making power over these businesses, enabling a few American politicians and lawyers to set the rules for how global businesses affect billions of people around the world. Platform socialists agree with the diagnosis of the new regulators but believe that the remedy required is a more thoroughgoing democratisation of the platform economy.

Platform socialism also has a more expansive ambition of targeting not only the largest platforms that would fall within the concept of a public utility but other platform companies as well. It's not only Facebook and Google that need to change, it's the structural factors determined by the capitalist economy itself that we need to challenge. Companies like Uber, Airbnb and Deliveroo could hardly be classified as utilities, but we have good reason to argue that these companies should also fall within our critique of the negative practices of platform businesses. The argument put forward in Chapter 5 is that new models of social ownership of digital platforms will better enable us to take back control of these services.

UNIVERSAL BASIC SERVICES

Making the case for the social ownership of digital platforms requires a renewed faith in the positive impact public services can have in spite of the neglect many have received in the neoliberal era of privatisation. There are many examples of well-functioning publicly owned services across the world. A prominent example that could be aspired to is the British National Health Service – a unifying point of universal admiration and acclaim for the British public. Despite its dire underfunding and ongoing partial privatisation by successive Conservative governments, the service it provides – universal care that is free at the point of use and publicly funded – is widely recognised as a modern marvel and the basis of a decent society. But it was incredibly radical and controversial at the time of its introduction. The Conservative Party voted against the Act 21 times before it was passed, while the British Medical Association vigorously opposed the institution, fearing attempts to cut into their profits and autonomy.[30] We should expect arguments for basic digital services to all citizens to be similarly opposed.

Another example is the highly efficient and publicly owned Swiss Federal Railway, the largest railway company in Switzerland, a country whose rail network was rated first in Europe according to the 2017 European Railway Performance Index.[31] Scottish Water is a publicly owned company answerable to Scottish ministers and is not only the most trusted utility in the United Kingdom but delivers cheaper bills and cleaner rivers than its English privately run counterparts.[32] In 2017, the Transnational Institute published a report detailing at least 835 examples of the remunicipalisation of public services that have occurred around the world since 2000.[33] This process of reclaiming critical services and network infrastructure is a growing trend from Germany to Latin America. Responding to the community's basic needs and environmental challenges, these services have been integrated back into public ownership, most often at the local level.

The idea that society should provide essential services to all regardless of wealth is not a radical idea. Polling in the UK consistently shows that the public ownership of water, energy, health and education is supported by a majority of the public.[34] There is no reason why the logic of these popular and successful ideas should not be extended to a range of other essential services, including those that could be offered in the digital sphere. In their book, *The Case for Universal Basic Services*, Anna Coote and Andrew Percy have argued that expanding the principle of basic service delivery to other everyday essentials like childcare and transport would provide a more efficient and practical way of organising these activities.[35] The British Labour Party supported the principle of universal connectivity by including free full fibre broadband to all in their 2019 election manifesto.[36] Essential digital services could also be run as part of public services that are provided free at the point of use and available to all citizens. This idea of universal basic services highlights the capacity for collectively funded services as the basis for a decent standard of living and for promoting solidarity and a common understanding of our shared resources.

Social ownership of digital platforms would enable the full potential of technology to be unleashed for the people. This transfer of wealth and power from the tech companies to the public would reverse the logic of privatisation that has pervaded the growth of technology over the past decades. Platforms should be repurposed so that the services do not extract wealth from communities but provide them with services that are free at the point of use and which generate value for the many.

DEMOCRACY AS AN INSURGENT MOVEMENT

Tech companies love to talk about democracy. Uber is democratising city transport; Airbnb is democratising travel; Deliveroo is democratising how we eat. When the tech industry promotes itself as a force for democracy what this usually means is that it wants more customers. Enhanced connectivity has increased people's access to a range of services and allowed more people than ever before to participate online. But we shouldn't confuse more users of a service as a win for democracy when the platforms themselves are still owned and controlled by a narrow oligarchic elite.

Let's disrupt the tech industry's idea of democracy with a little dose of the real thing. Unlike other forms of government, such as aristocracy and monarchy, which are based on the word ârche (to rule), democracy is based on the word *kratos*, meaning power. Scholars now believe that the original meaning of democracy to the Greeks meant something like 'the collective capacity of the people to act on matters of public concern'.[37] This is not simply the ability for everyone to use a company's service but to play an active role in shaping the basic institutions that govern their lives.

It's also worth remembering that democracy emerged in Athens as an insurgent movement against political and economic elites and their attempts to control society.[38] Cleisthenes' reforms to the Athenian polis in 508/7 BC undermined the domination of rival aristocratic families by creating a new partition of Athenian society into 139 districts called *demes*. This created a new basis for citizenship, made traditional bonds of deference politically irrelevant and broke apart the rule of a narrow clique of wealthy families. These democratic reforms disrupted the concentration of political power of elites through the creation of a new political community in which peasants and artisans were included. Citizenship was radically expanded to include 'subhoplite' (lower-class) natives as democratic citizens who could now participate in a deliberative popular assembly of the entire citizen body.

This injection of democracy into Athenian society meant that all citizens had an equal capacity to participate in deliberation and decision-making despite socio-economic inequalities. This radical principle was in opposition to those who thought decisions were best made by self-designated community leaders in the interests of the many. The aim was also to constrain elites from dominating politics, particularly because it was seen that their interests often conflicted with those of the lower classes. This is not to say that the system was without its faults. Athens still excluded women, slaves and non-citizens from participation, and wealthy families still exercised disproportionate power. But the Athenians' story of the rise of people power on the back of an insurgent movement for equality reminds us of the radical disruptive power of democracy, properly understood.

Some tech entrepreneurs may seem like liberal-minded oligarchs, but they are usurpers of public power all the same. Even if they make the occasional contribution to a progressive political movement or come out in support of a popular cause, the companies they preside over are little more than personal fiefdoms run in the interests of investors. The amount of direct power they exercise over decisions that affect the lives of billions of people should be more shocking than it often is. We need a new set of institutional arrangements that will guarantee the public rights of participation and control over the governance of digital platforms.

BIRMINGHAM TAKES BACK CONTROL

Public ownership over utilities has a long tradition which also serves as a useful resource for how predatory private companies can be transformed. Taking back control of our digital future might seem like an insurmountable task given the overwhelming power of the current tech giants, but there are historical precedents of private companies being reclaimed by the public. One prominent example is from the early 1870s when Joseph Chamberlain, the newly elected Liberal mayor of Birmingham, implemented a plan to purchase the city's two rival gas companies and the privately owned and poorly performing water company.[39] The city's water supply was a danger to public health and competition between the two gas companies had led to the city's streets being continually dug up to lay each company's lines. Birmingham's record on public health had fallen significantly by the 1860s, with problems in sanitation, disease and overcrowding. There was an emerging movement of a new kind of liberalism in the late nineteenth century that was critical of laissez faire economics and believed in public institutions playing a role in improving public health and well-being.

Rather than leaving large industries to the oligarchs for private profit, Chamberlain claimed, 'all monopolies which are in any way sustained by the State ought to be in the hands of the representations of the peoples – by the representative authority should they be administered, and to them should their profits go, and not to private speculators'.[40] Municipal control was also seen as an expansion of democracy and an increase in the power of local representatives elected by the people. Chamberlain wanted local authorities to become 'real local parliaments, supreme in their special jurisdiction'.[41]

Chamberlain organised for the public purchase of the companies and created new municipal institutions to administer them for the benefit of the public. Public ownership and provision was a huge success leading to lower rates for households, reduced gas leaks, less overheads and extra profits for the city. Public money was then used to construct new parks, libraries, schools, museums and swimming pools. Birmingham's 'gas and water' socialism emerged as an influential model for European and American reformers arguing for the democratic provision of public goods and services.[42] It gave birth to a number of experiments with public services which resisted privatisation across the UK, US and Europe. In the late nineteenth century, the Fabians believed they were experiencing an 'irresistible sweep' towards 'the control by the community of the means of production for public advantage, instead of for private profit'.[43]

What we can learn from these examples is that public ownership and provision make sense in industries with natural monopolies – high infrastructure costs or other barriers that give the largest supplier an overwhelming advantage. Where monopolies do develop, it provides opportunities for abuse and exploitative behaviour. Public utilities have been used throughout the world to run essential services such as water, electricity, transportation, postal services and mass communications. Publicly owned and community-run digital platforms are a natural extension of the principle of not allowing basic public services to be run for profit in a manner that exploits those who depend on them.

A LIBERTY MACHINE IN PROTOTYPE

We can also take inspiration from systems trialled in our recent past such as Chile's experiment with using technology to implement democratic control over its economy.[44] British cybernetics theorist Stafford Beer was the lead designer of Cybersyn, a project to assist the democratic management of Chile's economy through a network of telex machines and statistical modelling software. Salvador Allende had taken office in November 1970 and had nationalised key industries with the aim of increasing worker participation and control. Project Cybersyn was an attempt to put cybernetics – 'the science of effective organisation' concerned with the management of complex and adaptive systems – in the service of the Chilean people.

The system would provide real-time updates on factory production to a futuristic operations room that would facilitate comprehension of the data and help predict future economic activity. Masterfully reconstructed in Eden Medina's *Revolutionary Cybernetics*, the project represents an alternative tech-enabled future that produced a working prototype for national democratic economic management.[45] The 'liberty machine', as Beer dubbed it, was designed to enhance people's freedom through a socio-technical system that enabled greater direction and control over their material lives.

In its attempt to create a new system that allowed for greater worker participation and new forms of decentralised and adaptive control, Cybersyn provides an important point upon which we could pivot towards a new future. It enables us to destabilise the hegemonic position of Silicon Valley's privately owned future and imagine new possibilities. We can reorient to a world where technology is used by governments to expand the capacities of human freedom. Far from the totalitarian spectre that was imagined by the press at the time, Cybersyn was a humanist project to properly order the flows of information and feedback about economic life to put the direction of the economy back in the hands of democratic collectives.

In spite of Beer's good intentions of 'making the maximum effort towards the devolution of power', the resulting network resembled a technocratic approach to organisation which placed faith in the decision-making of technical experts at the higher levels of government.[46] His cybernetic management system allowed for workers' input to be filtered upwards, but there was no corresponding political arrangement for how such decision-makers could be held accountable and subject to democratic control from below. The hope was that national administrators would be benevolent and use the information to aid workers, but there was nothing stopping them from using this as a means of surveillance and control.

Rather than setting up a system of telex machines, we should be inspired by Cybersyn's unrealised aspirations for democratic transformation. It is striking how much was achieved with a relatively limited technical apparatus under adverse conditions. In a matter of months, the design team had produced a novel socio-technical system that represented a different configuration of political power to the command-and-control model of capitalist enterprises.

The individualism and competition at the heart of neoliberal capitalism has so thoroughly penetrated our understanding of tech products that we find it difficult to imagine how the two could be disentangled. The key for Beer was experimentation. New inventions had to be prototyped to enable learning from feedback loops as to how the system could be improved. In this way, systems need not be set in stone but could adapt and evolve by learning from data inputted through experience.

Cybersyn shows us that we need to act now to begin this process of participatory and decentralised experiments with our own digital platforms.

UNLEASHING COLLECTIVE INNOVATION

Opponents of public ownership see this as stifling innovation in the sector by locking in one set of tools and preventing the competition necessary for further growth. The idea that public ownership leads to bureaucratic inefficiency and waste is so deeply embedded in our economic common sense that it is simply accepted by most as a truism. However, a systematic review of the evidence demonstrates that this has more to do with a successful public relations campaign by the New Right in the postwar era and a Cold War mindset that opposes Soviet-style centralised planning. Andrew Cumbers has shown that the empirical evidence is varied and does not point to either private or public ownership as uniformly more efficient.[47] In a 2007 report for the United Nations, Cambridge economist Ha-Joon Chang found that state-owned enterprises did not underperform their privately owned counterparts.[48] In the UK, the nationalised utilities in transport and communications frequently outperformed their privately owned companies in the United States during the postwar period.[49]

Far from stifling innovation, public digital services would provide an enormous boost to research and new advances in the sector. We should put to rest the tired cliché of the lumbering bureaucratic state and the agile and dynamic private sector. One of the greatest myths of the tech sector is that we owe it all to the genius of a bunch of young male entrepreneurs. The dominant narrative of entrepreneurial-driven innovation ignores the fact that the success of these individuals was only possible by building on the publicly funded, collective and cumulative nature of research and innovation.

In *The Entrepreneurial State*, Professor Mariana Mazzucato has shown that every piece of technology that makes the iPhone so innovative – its use of the internet, touchscreen, voice-activated software and GPS system – has been created through public funding.[50] She demonstrates that in the digital economy the risks of innovation are shouldered by the public, while the rewards of small breakthroughs are hoarded by private companies. The huge profits of tech companies are only possible on the basis of collective value creation through public research. Many of the biggest and most widely used innovations were supported by government funding into research and development. From the internet to super computers, magnetic resonance imaging, smartphones, civilian aviation, LED lighting, prosthetics and nanotech, it is the public sector that funds the exploratory, high-risk innovation that has made the biggest technological advances. The digital network created by affordable home computers, the internet and the world wide web was made possible by research from the US Department of Defense, CERN, research universities and years of collaborative research. It was built on a policy of open access and free use.

A capitalist patenting system has ensured that the value of societal innovations has largely been captured by a few individuals.[51] Patents tend to extract value rather than create it and can even inhibit further innovation by closing down the 'open science' model in which research outcomes are available to all. Acknowledging the true collective and cumulative nature of innovation allows for a more efficient and publicly beneficial financing of the process. Entrepreneurs within a capitalist system succeed by entering at just the right time when high-risk and low-reward aspects of the research have already been undertaken by other actors. Private entrepreneurs can enter sectors late in order to stand on the shoulders of previous research and privatise the rewards at the moment it becomes profitable to develop a product ready for market. The result is that huge amounts of taxpayers' money are funnelled into for-profit enterprises which are then locked away in private fortunes.

Public investment would change the incentive structure for investment from value capture towards value creation. It would recognise that innovation is uncertain and that most attempts at developing new research will not produce immediate and direct results. Removing the incentive for immediate marketisation and the quick move to an IPO sell-off would expand the possibilities for research development. Governments supporting public platforms should invest heavily in research and development to ensure continual innovation in the digital sector. This will drive designers and developers to produce publicly useful apps and systems that fulfil important social needs rather than those that can capture the most value from social activity.

Social ownership and control over investment in technology would also ensure that when long-term investments did bear fruit it would be the public who would benefit. It is likely that this enhanced public role of investing in technology would have enormous flow-on effects to the rest of the economy. Nobel Prize winner Robert Solow has shown that developments in technology explained over 80 per cent of economic growth in the US from 1909 to 1949.[52] A new golden era in publicly backed technological development would be a boon for the global economy currently experiencing high levels of economic stagnation and low rates of investment and job creation.

OURS TO MASTER AND TO CODE

One major concern is that public ownership of digital platforms would place large amounts of personal data in the government's hands which would be a threat to citizens' individual liberties. Do we really want to replace Zuckerberg and Bezos with Biden and Bolsonaro? Would this not just provide the government – an institution well known for its history of surveillance, violence and discrimination – with access to our most personal information and activities?

Calls for democratisation need not involve an overly centralised model of state command-and-control similar to twentieth-century versions of state socialism in the USSR and China. Instead, we can turn to new forms of social ownership that could be dispersed across the local, regional, national and international levels. The aim is not to transfer power from private to public elites but to democratise ownership and empower people to participate in new structures of governance.

It's important to note that there is no foolproof system that can immunise politics from corruption and abuse. Any system involves the vesting of authoritative decision-making power in certain organisations and positions, which inevitably leads to trade-offs in terms of how to ensure popular empowerment and effective accountability. Our goal should be democratisation and the decentralisation of power to place it back in the hands of ordinary people. The more that power shifts from elected governments to private corporations, the less opportunity democratic citizens have to hold them to account. The ongoing privatisation of public infrastructure and services removes the thin layer of accountability still available within liberal democracies, however imperfectly this currently functions.

The answer to concerns about state abuse of power is not to pass the buck to even less accountable private corporations but to push for the further democratisation of society. Institutions which govern our everyday lives – from national governments to local councils, housing organisations and social media platforms – should be opened to participatory mechanisms that enable ordinary citizens to influence their decision-making.

Social ownership also need not entail the government having access to large amounts of personal data. Administrative bodies can be established at arm's length from the executive of the government with special protections and restrictions placed on citizens' data. Legislation would need to be passed by states to establish regulations for the new status of certain digital platforms, but this doesn't entail executive branches of government having access to and control over large amounts of private information. It's false to assume that we face a binary choice between completely unaccountable private oligarchs on the one hand and a Stasi-like state-run Big Brother operation on the other.

The principle we need to support is the strengthening of democratic popular sovereignty in the face of the rising power of tech oligarchs. The central problem of the tech sector today is not one that any technological fix can remedy. It is primarily a problem of inequalities of power that have arisen due to the rise of private empires within the platform economy. Platform socialism aims to equalise power between citizens and to counteract the hierarchies that emerge due to social and economic inequalities. The answer to many of the problems of the tech industry is to subject these powerful companies to greater democratic oversight and control.

5
Guild Socialism for the Digital Economy

To develop the principles and institutional sketch of platform social-ism I draw inspiration from the writings of two early twentieth-century writers: the libertarian socialist G. D. H. Cole and the Austrian philos-opher and economist Otto Neurath. These two figures are seldom read today, even on the Left, but their ideas motivate a fresh approach to thinking about the digital economy.

Cole joined the Fabian Society during his university years but became a critic of its top-down nationalisation strategies and lack of support for workplace democracy.[1] His writings enable us to envision the platform economy as a federal network of democratic associations governed by active citizens. They also include valuable reflections on how workers' control over the labour process can be balanced with the interests of broader community participation.

Otto Neurath became a member of the German Social Democratic Party during the German Revolution of 1918–19 and was in charge of the central economic planning office in Munich during the short-lived Bavarian Soviet Republic.[2] He offers important insight into economic planning and how resources could be allocated democratically through deliberation on the common good.

The chapter reconstructs key aspects of their political and economic thought and translates them into proposals for digital platforms. His-torian of political thought Quentin Skinner has argued that, 'once a political idea achieves a position of hegemony it comes to be regarded as the only coherent way of thinking about the concept involved'.[3] Reflect-ing on different historical approaches to organising the economy reveals how 'our present ways of thinking ... reflect a series of choices made at different times between different possible worlds'. Returning to these writers helps denaturalise current hegemonic accounts of technology and opens up new ways of thinking about our digital future.

G. D. H. COLE'S DEMOCRATIC ASSOCIATIONALISM

Cole's criticism of existing democratic societies begins with the following insight:

> Society will be in health only if it is in the full sense democratic and self-governing, which implies not only that all the citizens should have a 'right' to influence its policy if they so desire, but that the greatest possible opportunity should be afforded for every citizen actually to exercise this right.[4]

Guild socialists like Cole believed that the current political and economic institutional arrangements impeded individuals from exercising their full capacities as democratic citizens. He wondered why we would demand democracy in the political sphere of government but 'totally ignore the effects of undemocratic organisation and convention in non-political spheres of social action' such as workplaces.[5] In response to this democratic deficit, he proposed that every important association should have its own democratic structure of governance: from universities and schools to businesses and economic regulatory institutions. If citizens had the right to elect a member of parliament, they should also have the right to elect representatives in their workplaces and other associations.

We find in Cole's writings an intriguing theory of *democratic associationalism*, in which cooperation rather than force is seen as the mechanism that enables people to build organisations and work towards shared goals. It is a reflection upon 'the motives that hold men together in association' and the 'way in which men act through associations in supplement and complement to their actions as isolated or private individuals'.[6] Cole considered that for individuals to remain self-governing as members of these associations, they should have participatory rights in decision-making over their structure and purpose.

He argued that society was divided into different functional social systems, each with their own various associations. The driving force of Cole's guild socialism was the desire to institute what he called a 'functional democracy' in different domains of social life. This was an idea of democracy understood not simply as a set of abstract rights but in terms of real participation and involvement in the most important associations that governed individuals' everyday lives. He believed that 'democracy is only real when it is conceived in terms of function and purpose'.[7] Democratic principles should be instituted within associations to ensure that they served their members effectively and provided a genuine benefit to the community.

He called for a participatory democracy in which multiple and overlapping producer, consumer and municipal associations coordinated social life. In Cole's sketch in *Guild Socialism Restated*, he envisioned cultural councils organising art galleries, museums and libraries; education guilds organising schools, universities and other tertiary institutions; health guilds; collective utilities councils; industrial councils; civil service councils; consumer councils; and co-operative councils. All of these democratic organisations would be integrated through a central coordinating body he called the National Commune. The underlying idea was to extend democratic principles of citizen control and autonomy from the narrow political sphere of the state to broader social life. This vision of a radical democratic future entailed a greater emphasis on distributed forms of governance, a participatory political culture and citizens exercising meaningful democratic control over their lives.

DECENTRING THE STATE

Cole's theory required a decentralisation of power throughout society. He argued that the power and authority of the state should be drastically reduced to a coordinating agency – one small element in a larger social system of internally democratic associations led by active citizens. The state was just one association among others and to consider it the only home for democracy was to ignore the reality of the diverse range of democratic practices that could be expanded and institutionalised. Sovereignty was best conceived as belonging to the whole community and divided throughout its many associations, leading to different spheres of authority and democratic action. The problem with the fiction of what Cole called the 'omnicompetent state' was that it had monopolised authority over multiple social spheres without the corresponding structures to exercise this authority in a democratic manner. The state was poorly equipped to enable citizens to exercise meaningful control over important social institutions in their lives due to its size, bureaucracy and militarisation. For Cole, the powerful and bureaucratic state apparatus had no place in a truly self-governing community. It had usurped the functions of the overlapping authority structures of the pre-modern period and driven Europe into the First World War.

Cole represented what Mark Bevir has called a 'distinctive socialist tradition of pluralism' within early twentieth-century British politics which challenged the state's centralisation of power and the tendency of socialists to think of socialisation exclusively in state terms.[8] The pluralist agenda of this associationalism posed a radical alternative to Fabianism and the various forms of state socialism of the era. In the first three decades of the twentieth century the main division of the British Labour Party was between a liberal representative concept of democracy and a participatory and pluralist alternative. The liberal model sought to protect citizens from the actions of government whereas the participatory approach considered that citizens should have as much control as possible over the institutions that governed their daily lives. Democracy needed to be a principle enacted from the bottom up in workplaces and local councils across the country. The vast reduction in the role of the state should be accompanied by an increase in the power of smaller associations which would play a more active role in self-government. The argument for a strong centralised state won the debate within the Labour Party, cementing itself after the 1945 Labour electoral victory and marginalising the more decentralist and municipalist traditions within the party.

GUILDS AND COMMUNITY CONTROL

The term 'guilds' evokes an image of the mediaeval institutions which organised small-scale production and can give the theory of guild socialism a nostalgic and impractical feel. But Cole was more interested with the underlying idea of restoring power to individuals rather than any specific institutional feature of the former guild system. Far from seeking to restore older ways of life, the idea behind Cole's modern guild system was to institute forms of self-government directly into workplaces within industrial production. In Cole's theory, guilds were democratic associations based on the unit of the workplace or factory and extended to larger guilds of industries. They would provide 'the greatest possible extension of local initiative and of autonomy for the small group' while allowing coordination between units in higher councils. For example,

the Railway Guild would include all the workers of every type – from general managers and technicians to porters and engine cleaners required for the conduct of the railways as a public service. This association would be entrusted by the community with the duty and responsibility of administering the railways efficiently for the public benefit, and would be left itself to make the internal arrangements for the running of trains and to choose its own officers, administrators, and methods of organisation.[9]

Cole's version of guild socialism can be differentiated from the more authoritarian models offered by S. G. Hobson and Ramiro de Maeztu who believed large systems of national guilds should monopolise the supply of labour and control industry in cooperation with the state. Cole differed significantly from other guild theorists in terms of his support for the freedom of individuals. In contrast to the more collectivist leanings of other guild theorists, Cole believed that the purpose of the guild system was to enable each individual to flourish and participate in a self-governing community. By 1920, the mature statement of his theory in *Guild Socialism Restated* included a wide variety of councils to deepen participatory democracy at a local level. For Cole, the central concept was 'community control' – how interconnected individuals working towards a common cause could regain collective self-determination over their economic and political institutions.

BEYOND NATIONALISATION

The first question these ideas help us address is how digital platforms could be owned and operated. Platform socialism would need to innovate beyond the top-down managerial forms of nationalisation of the postwar era. Transferring ownership of a company to the state does not guarantee greater worker participation or democracy in the workplace.[10] In fact, when we look at the options for democratic ownership and control more closely, there are two equally problematic alternatives to be avoided: *exclusive workers' control* and *top-down nationalisation.*[11]

In the first case, workplaces would be handed over to their workers to own and manage. The problem with this approach is that vast inequalities would emerge between workers in different industries. Furthermore, an even bigger inequality would emerge between those engaged in full-time paid work and others who undertook unpaid, voluntary and care work (or for various reasons didn't work at all). Turning over Alphabet to its 132,000 employees would be great for them, but what about the rest of the global community? The concern is that workers left to control individual firms could potentially ignore the interests of others and engage in price gouging or monopoly/rent-seeking behaviour.[12]

However, we also need to ensure that democratising the digital economy does not end in a bureaucratic autocracy in which power is placed exclusively in the hands of the state and national managers. Many twentieth-century attempts at nationalisation were top-down efforts that did not provide enough scope for true community engagement. Even the Swedish Meidner Plan – which would have transferred ownership of large corporations to employees – was planned to be controlled by big unions rather than the workers themselves.[13] With an absence of grass-roots participation, nationalisation simply replaces private oligarchs with distant bureaucrats.

Guild theory points us towards a focus on the functions performed by each platform and the need to build structures of democratic governance that reflect these. We should strive for a pluralist approach to democratic platform governance in which the ownership and management of platforms are undertaken at a variety of levels: local, regional, national and international. Democratic platforms should be governed by a principle of subsidiarity – services should be delivered by the most local and proximate level that would be able to undertake the task efficiently, sustainably and in a manner that would maximise its benefit for users. Even in cases where the state or a municipal body owns the productive assets in question, service delivery could be democratically managed by those most affected at a community level. The overarching objective should be for the democratic control of digital platforms with questions of whether this should be undertaken at a municipal, regional or national level best determined through practical experience.

Finding a way to democratise the tech world of mega platforms and multi-billion dollar empires will involve a radical rethink of the size and scale of our existing models. It may be in the interests of investors to blitzscale platforms to global dimensions but this doesn't always serve the interests of the communities that use them. It used to be a warning of the dangers of communism that we would all be forced to buy our goods from one supplier. Yet this is precisely what has occurred with today's global platform monopolies of Amazon, Facebook and Google. Cole argued that many of the services that had been usurped by the state were in fact better performed at a local and regional level. The same is true for certain platform companies related to location-based service delivery.

How this would work in practice would depend on the industry. We could imagine businesses like domestic cleaning, courier services, freelance labourers, handywork and other such activities being owned and operated by local worker-owned businesses. For short-term rental platforms, app-based ride hail services and food delivery platforms, there is a strong case that these would be more appropriately managed at the municipal or city level. At the next level, healthcare, childcare and social security could be provided by state or national governments. There are other global services, however, which would be difficult to decentralise without destroying the fundamental benefit the service brings. In this category, we can place social network platforms and internet search engines, which are international in their scope and operation. At each stage we should think of the function the platform performs and the communities that are affected by the actions of the association.

DEMOCRATISING THE PLATFORM

At the level of the firm that owns and operates a digital platform, worker control should be instituted to redistribute power and give workers strong democratic rights over the labour process and the strategic direction of the firm. Small worker-controlled platforms could have their assets owned by the workers themselves as in a traditional worker co-operative. Another possible arrangement would be for assets to be distributed between workers and other stakeholders such as users, consumers, municipal authorities and larger associations as part of a social ownership scheme. This would break the power of large-scale investment funds in determining the direction of multinational corporations acting solely in the pursuit of shareholder value.

Social ownership of digital platforms should also be combined with new structures of democratic governance. Most matters internal to the functioning of the platform should be in the direct control of workers who would democratically elect a board through a system of one worker, one vote. However, platforms are designed to connect different parties and create common interests around members' shared needs. Digital platforms blur the lines between worker-owned, consumer-owned and community-owned associations precisely because they tend to create value from people who are not traditional employees of the company. Multi-stakeholder governance would therefore be suitable in many cases, which could include consumers/users and other groups affected by the actions of the firm. For example, Resonate is a stream-to-own music platform and multi-stakeholder co-operative which divides its governance between artists (45 per cent), listeners (35 per cent) and workers (20 per cent).[14] Hybrid models of representing stakeholder interests might also lead to specific roles and rights for different types of members.

These changes in ownership and governance would provide a new purpose for digital platforms and change fundamental aspects about how they operate. The incentive for boards of platform companies would be to serve members and the public rather than maximising profit and providing strong returns to institutional shareholders. Rather than maximising engagement with the platform and designing the product around advertisers' needs, platforms could be directed towards improving the health and well-being of their workers and users. The coordination rights of the company would be more equitably distributed among various stakeholders and would be held and exercised in common. Worker ownership over local platforms would also ensure that value generated by the platform was distributed to workers and those impacted by the platform's activities. Drawing on Cole's idea of a participatory society of active citizens, we could imagine a thriving platform ecosystem of different-sized associations that are socially owned, are democratically managed and provide benefits for their members and the public.

REPRESENTATION ON PLATFORMS

But does anybody really want to participate in the governance of every platform they use? Isn't the problem with these types of proposals that they simply take up too many evenings? Drawing on Cole, we can see that this need not be the case. Members can retain rights to exercise power at crucial moments when they want to, and can delegate many questions of day-to-day governance to a democratically elected board. Cole was in favour of greater participation, but he also saw the benefits of a representative system if it was suitably reformed. His central insight was that representatives in the political sphere could never adequately represent their electorate 'as a whole' because it contained too many different complex social systems which required their own democratic structures. The representation offered by liberal democracy was illusory because as more and more of social life was brought under the control of the state, representatives tasked with representing voters on an innumerably large number of different issues ceased to have any real relation to their constituency. There were also a vast number of institutions outside of government that played an important role in everyday life which had no representative structures and were run in an oligarchic manner. Representation for Cole should be 'specific and functional' rather than 'general and inclusive'.[15] Citizens should be able to elect representatives in relation to each of the major functional organisations to which they belonged to represent them for a particular purpose.

Cole also thought that democratic representation required electors to have more practical control over their representatives. Citizens require more robust accountability mechanisms than simply the power to vote a representative out at infrequent intervals. He called for more contact between electors and representatives and for electors to exercise 'considerable control over' their representatives.[16] Cole held a view of representation more akin to what we would now call a 'delegate' model of representation, according to which representatives must vote in line with the views of their constituents rather than being authorised to act on the basis of their own judgement. In variations on this model, delegates can sometimes be bound by *imperative mandates* to vote in a specific way, or they could be subject to the *right of immediate recall* if they fail to act in the interests of their electors. The right of recall has been a common feature of workers' organisations throughout the history of the workers' movement.

Members should be able to exercise their rights over important issues they care about without necessarily voting on every small issue. They would not need to be involved in every decision but require the power to contest important decisions made by their representatives. If power remains with the membership and there are appropriate accountability mechanisms built into the design of platform governance, then members of platforms would be able to retain control over important matters.

THE RETURN OF POLITICS

A significant limitation of these libertarian socialist visions of post-capitalist society was their tendency to believe that the end of capitalism would usher in the end of political disagreement and conflict. This anti-political tendency in the literature was based on the idea that without a capitalist system of exploitation and domination a different kind of human being would begin to flourish that would have a much greater inclination for cooperative behaviour. Cole wanted to reduce as much as possible the need for coercive instruments in society and sought to abolish the standing army and the police force as we know it. For Cole,

> We want to build a new Society which will be conceived in the spirit, not of coercion, but of free service, and in the belief, not that men must be driven, but that they are capable of leading themselves, if the conditions of democratic fellowship are assured. ... In relation to the individual, the difficulty is not to provide Society with the means of coercion, but to prevent it from employing the means it possesses far too stringently and often.[17]

He recognised that the coercion of individuals to follow the community's laws would ultimately be necessary, but saw coercion as something to be reduced through the harmonising of interests and the reduction of relationships of domination in society.

One element that we should like to add to Cole's political thought is stronger protections for civil liberties and a more robust constitutional system to maintain the central administrative and judicial structures of society. Cole, like many libertarian socialists and anarchists, conceptualised post-capitalist society in terms of coordination problems rather than endemic conflict and political disagreement. There is a certain naivety here, as noted by Marxist intellectual Henry Pachter: 'It seems to them that under socialism people will undergo a fundamental change of character; not being alienated, they will have neither different interests nor different opinions, but will gladly cooperate in any reasonable assignment that the government decides upon.'[18] The persistence of political differences and deep antagonisms about how society should be organised means we need to imagine a post-capitalist society without the ideal of a harmonious natural order and the absence of coercive institutions. The democratisation of the economic sphere should also be embedded in a constitutional-legal structure that secures the powers of diverse associations and provides the institutional structure for democratic self-government.

DEMOCRATIC PLANNING

In addition to this organisational model of overlapping voluntary associations in the digital economy related to production and service delivery, we also need a way to tackle big system-level challenges related to investment and the allocation of resources. Without the private ownership of capital goods invested to make a profit we would require some form of economic planning to determine how goods would be put to use. But how would such a system of planning be devised and implemented?

Marx wrote little about the nature of a socialist society, but one of his clearest statements was in *Capital* where he described a post-capitalist economy as 'production by freely associated men ... consciously regulated by them in accordance with a settled plan'.[19] He contrasted the anarchy of production for profit with a rational and planned economy. Marxists all tended to share the view that a socialist society would replace private ownership and market forces with social ownership and planned production, but few thought it necessary to explain how this would work in practice.

One figure to have contributed to this task was Otto Neurath. Marxists, in his view, had been inattentive to how a rational system of social planning would be organised. He thought that planning had to be system-wide and applied to national economies, pointing to the limitations of democracy being gradually introduced to only limited sectors of the economy such as plans to nationalise the coal mines and certain other industrial sectors in Germany following the 1918–19 Revolution.[20] There was little point in achieving small pockets of co-operative production when the main sources of society's wealth remained in the hands of elites. Well known during his lifetime for his theory of 'total socialization', Neurath considered that 'socialism cannot be realised in parts of the economy: it presupposes the reshaping of the entire economic order'.[21]

His idea was that the allocation of society's resources should be a matter consciously decided upon by the entire people and not left to the anarchic forces of the market or to the self-interested machinations of oligarchs. Society should have the opportunity to deliberate over the best allocation of resources with different groups able to put forth their point of view and discuss the relative benefits of increasing investment in one sector of the economy or another. He thought people should consider different economic plans with various distributions of investment and choose the one that produced the maximum quality of life for them. Although an unlimited number of alternatives would theoretically be possible, a planning board could prepare several characteristic proposals and put them to deliberation and a popular vote.

For Neurath, economic planning wasn't simply a matter of optimising for efficiency in production. At different points in economic life, we freely disregard profit maximisation as the only or most important goal. Schools, hospitals and museums are not built to yield profit and are judged on their contribution to the public good. In choosing between different plans we should employ a kind of 'social Epicureanism' that inquires about the overall happiness and well-being of human beings. Neurath asked: 'what is the effect of different orders of life, of different measures, on the conditions of life of human beings and thereby on their happiness and unhappiness?'[22] He stressed that decisions about the allocation of resources called for ethical and political decisions about different forms of life. It would be necessary to make qualitative judgements for which no scientific calculation was possible. How reliant should we be on fossil fuels versus investing in research towards alternative sources of energy? How much should we invest in education or the arts compared to social care and welfare?

If we were in charge of how society's resources are invested we would be called on to actively shape our own world. One of the most urgent questions would be addressing the climate emergency and dramatically reducing our impact on the environment. The crisis of our global climate system means we only have a few short years to dramatically cut CO_2 emissions to avoid 1.5°C warming.[23] The failure to take serious action on climate change is already resulting in countries, particularly those in the Global South, being hit by cyclones, droughts and other extreme weather conditions. Democratic planning would give us the tools of public investment to adapt our economy through a green industrial strategy and rapidly transition away from harmful and extractive practices that are destroying the basis for natural life.

Democratically allocating resources would also involve questions of how much we wanted to work and how much time we wanted to collectively devote to other activities. Any long-term plan for a just and sustainable economy would need to involve a reduction in the time we spend working.[24] Given greater control over how their work is organised, many people would choose to simply work less or to reorganise their jobs to reduce the need for necessary labour time. Diminishing the burden of work would enable us to pursue a wide variety of other activities through joining with others in voluntary associations. Our investment programme could include far greater scope for social enrichment programmes so more people can learn new skills, socialise together, play games and explore new aspects of their world.

PLANNING THE FUTURE

Neurath imagined an economic plan as a blueprint or vision for a particular way of life. We wouldn't have to work out every precise detail or have a complete list of exactly how many products each economic unit should produce. The plan would enable us to be self-determining over the material conditions of our lives at a macro level without requiring the kind of centralised command economy of the Soviet Union. Underlying Neurath's work is the distinction between directive and indicative planning. In the former, a central authority would give orders as to how much every subordinate organisation needed to produce, whereas indicative planning is about setting targets and directing resources into broad sectors while allowing for a degree of autonomy in fulfilling these objectives. It would 'serve much more like a framework within which specific measures are carried out'.[25] The plan might also be accompanied by policies intended to show how certain core objectives could be fulfilled.

Some of Neurath's contemporaries understood him as advocating for a top-down model of a command economy.[26] While it is true that a strong modernist and centralising spirit pervades the majority of late nineteenth- and early twentieth-century socialist writing – including Neurath's – his system of planning allows for a much greater degree of plurality. As he responded to critics, planning can 'enable us to be free to an extent hardly heard before, "free" i.e. a multiplicity of ways of life possible, non-conformism supported by planned institutions'.[27] Neurath allowed for what he called 'economic tolerance' – not every facet of the economy needed to be bent to the will of a master plan. He presumed there would be small pockets of alternative economic modes of life within society that would not undermine the functioning of the system as a whole. A plan would allow for a pluralist economy in which a diversity of economic forms could flourish based on democratic deliberation and decision-making.

Not every aspect of Neurath's economic theory is worth returning to today. He believed that a socialist economy should be moneyless and without any markets for either production or consumer goods. He called for an 'economics in kind' that did not rely on money calculations but rather tabulated the precise quantities of different materials available within the economy. For Neurath, a socialist economy would implement an economic plan, 'without using profit and loss accounting, without circulation of money – be it metal or labour money – without using a common unit of calculation at all'.[28] This would require a new 'universal statistics' that would 'track the individual raw materials overall, by attempting to capture import, export, production (transformation), consumption and stockpiling for all forms of raw materials'.[29] German sociologist and political economist Max Weber rightly pointed out that while this may have been possible in household economies and certain small-scale moneyless economies in ancient societies, this technique was inadequate to meet the demands of mass production and consumption typical of modern societies.[30] To best fulfil Neurath's desire for democratic planning, complex societies would require monetary calculations to understand and interrogate the relative costs associated with different plans and judge between them.

SOCIALISING CAPITAL FUNDS

In our current system, stock ownership is concentrated in the funds of giant asset managers who hold fully diversified portfolios on behalf of institutional investors. Over the past 30 years there has been a reconcentration of share ownership, which has gradually solidified into a new regime of 'asset manager capitalism'.[31] Large digital platforms are predominantly funded by a venture capital model which promotes risk-taking and ambitions for monopolisation.

The movement towards democratic planning would require the socialisation of large capital funds to be repurposed to serve the common good. In the short term, we can look to leverage existing public and semi-public pools of capital such as pension funds to impose social constraints on investment. Postwar management guru Peter Drucker saw that an increasing share of global capital was now indirectly owned by workers through pension schemes, which could be directed through a form of 'pension fund socialism'.[32] We could also turn to ideas for 'wage-earner funds' such as the proposed Meidner Plan in 1980s Sweden or the British Labour Party's proposal for an Inclusive Ownership Fund, established through the gradual transfer of a portion of the shares of large companies to be managed for payouts to employees.[33] But, in the long term, larger sources of capital would need to be targeted. Three asset managers – Vanguard, BlackRock and State Street Global Advisors – now control more than US$15 trillion, making them the largest shareholders of 88 per cent of firms in the S&P 500.[34]

Some critics of Big Tech have suggested that dominant platform companies could be adequately constrained from engaging in harmful practices through greater government regulation rather than the socialisation of capital. It is possible to imagine some publicly regulated platforms operating within a social democratic system of a mixed economy in which the majority of capital was still privately controlled. However, by seeking to tame rather than fundamentally transform capitalism, this social democratic alternative leaves the majority of power still in the hands of private investors who resent the constraints placed on them by democratic government. If we look at historical examples of the radical edges of social democracy in terms of employee ownership schemes and gradualist plans for socialisation – the Mitterand government in the early 1980s and the Meidner Plan in Sweden – these were brought to a halt by threatened or actual capital strikes. With capitalists still in charge of the economy, there are limits to what a political democracy can do if capital refuses to make investments and sabotages the project.

Trillions of dollars of private capital are managed by institutional investors and asset managers, which places enormous economic power in the hands of a select few. The socialisation of these large pools of capital could open up new avenues for these funds to be used to finance ambitious infrastructure projects, provide grants for local businesses and promote just and sustainable investment in socially useful projects. Requirements to provide good jobs, a sustainable and equitable business model and social value could be written into the conditions of investment in enterprises.

COORDINATION ACROSS PLATFORMS

One issue with planning is the unavoidable tension between worker-controlled enterprises and system-wide planning. In capitalism, this issue does not arise because all investment decisions are made by private entities without any regard for broader social concerns. Neurath's instinct was towards a centralised model because of his insistence that the 'power of the workers is decisive not within the factory, but within the people's economy as a whole'.[35] However, he still believed planning would enable 'the enlivening activity of smaller groups and associations' and that their relationship with the central administration would be 'conciliatory and not despotic'.[36] Even though worker control over the labour process is not emphasised in his writings, this idea – which comes out strongly in Cole's theory – can find a place within Neurath's planning system. Neurath greatly admired Cole's writings and, despite certain disagreements, wanted to combine his associational theory with a more explicit emphasis on economic planning.

In Cole's theory, disagreements between democratic associations over the demarcation of power and responsibility could be resolved by deliberation and, in the final instances, by the coordinating body of the National Commune. This body would also be in charge of the allocation of resources in dialogue with the various guilds. The guilds would prepare budgets of which resources they required in consultation with other guilds, which the National Commune would then 'bring into harmony', as Cole puts it, with the estimated resources available and expected national production.

Expanding upon this basic idea, we arrive at a broader notion of *participatory planning*, a system through which different associations engage in negotiated coordination as to how resources could be most effectively allocated between them.[37] Associations would already have a general idea of how economy-wide priorities had been set for that economic cycle and could make plans for distributing production goods between different groups in their region and industry. Decisions about allocation would be made to satisfy people's needs and consumer demands rather than being the unplanned outcome of different organisations' desires to maximise profit on their investment. This negotiation would cover issues such as where new infrastructure was needed, how new processes and techniques of production could be developed and how different groups could best meet the overarching strategic goals of the plan. While there would be no market in production goods (material needed for further economic production activity), markets in consumer goods could still provide indicators as to what types of goods people wanted and how different associations could best satisfy these needs. This system of negotiated coordination would need to take place at a range of different levels, from municipal and regional councils to national and international ones.

HAYEK'S CRITIQUE OF SOCIALIST PLANNING

Any proposal for public ownership and democratic planning needs to contend with the influential critique offered by Friedrich Hayek –

often thought to be devastating to the socialist cause.[38] It is of particular concern here because Neurath was one of the main targets of Hayek's critique. Hayek's writings were so influential that by the end of the century even many 'market socialists' - as they now called themselves - framed their arguments in terms of his insights into price signals and market systems.[39] Hayek's argument against central planning in his book, *The Road to Serfdom*, was that despite the good intentions of planners, a system involving a central planning agency would inevitably lead to the centralisation of power and decision-making, destroying individual freedom and democracy in the process.[40] His fear was that would-be social democratic planners in western Europe would turn their countries into totalitarian dictatorships through submitting all individuals to the authority of a central planning board in the service of abstract notions of the common good and social justice.

While these political criticisms of central planning had the largest impact, the cornerstone of his critique of socialism can be found in his earlier economic arguments about the superiority of markets over central planning in coordinating the economic activity of different individuals with local and often tacit knowledge of their own unique situations.[41] He claimed that no planning agency could ever gather all the necessary information required to make rational economic decisions because a well-functioning economy depended on individual actors continually making on-the-spot judgements based on evolving market factors.

Hayek framed this aspect of his argument in epistemological rather than political terms. The real problem with planning, he insisted, was the dispersion of local knowledge throughout society. Markets proved highly advantageous because they enabled participants to coordinate their actions and respond to surpluses and shortages by following the signals of the price system without ever having full knowledge of the entire situation.

Hayek considered the price system to be a 'marvel' because of its purported rational utilisation of resources in spite of local knowledge being dispersed among many actors. Market prices are essential for entrepreneurs because they enable them to choose the most efficient means of investing their capital and provide incentives for them to create new products and discover innovative ways of operating. Hayek's emphasis on the 'spontaneous order' of the market challenged the modernist faith many Marxists had in the capacity for human beings to consciously and rationally organise human society to meet basic needs.

PLANNING AFTER HAYEK

It would be a mistake to assume that the only possible response to Hayek would be one that largely accepted his terms of debate. We do not face a binary choice between rigid centralised planning and an idealised free market society for coordinating economic life. There is not one kind of 'free market' but many variations depending on how we regulate them and enable different structural possibilities. Furthermore, Hayek's characterisation of socialism as a Soviet-style central planning board with near total power over individuals and institutions to conform to a strict plan also fails to consider the possibility of discursive non-market alternatives in the form of deliberation and negotiation between decentralised organisations.

A response to Hayek's criticisms should begin by agreeing with the need for a commitment to pluralism and the concern for the dangers of centralised power. In fact, these criticisms can be directed back to the very system Hayek defends. In the digital economy, tech founders have amassed such enormous power that the decisions of a single individual can now affect billions of people across the globe. Questions of the design of products, the rules of conduct for the digital public sphere and how we access information are all made by a tiny handful of actors based on what appears most profitable for their companies rather than of value to society. The dominance of tech monopolies resulting from current conditions gives us reason to doubt that the free market alternative fully delivers on its commitment to promoting pluralism and individual freedoms.

It is clear that Hayek offers an overly idealised account of markets and underplays the negative effect of externalities, imperfect market conditions, inequalities in access to information and the poverty and precarity markets can produce. But perhaps most egregiously, Hayek's system ignores the power structures that exist between different economic actors and the vast inequalities in wealth and capital that determine who can make important decisions in a market economy. Only a small handful of powerful firms are able to engage in decision-making over questions of production, leaving most actors in a position where they are forced to sell their labour, trapped within the oligarchic structure of the modern firm. As economist Pat Devine has argued,

> a major weakness in the modern Austrian School's emphasis on the need for tacit knowledge to be socially mobilised by entrepreneurs

participating in the market process is that participation is restricted to those with access to capital, thus ignoring the tacit knowledge of the majority of people.[42]

Another problematic aspect of Hayek's model of market-based coordination is that it is entirely non-discursive, leaving no room for rational deliberation, compromise and mutually beneficial agreements. Price signals may communicate *something* to entrepreneurs but their knowledge of what has occurred is extremely limited. A system of participatory planning could allow for a degree of discussion and debate over how to approach certain economic problems and enable social coordination to take place as a result of conscious choices rather than economic actors trying to second-guess the reason behind shifts in prices.

Participatory planning today can also take advantage of the mass participatory tools enabled through digital technology that could help facilitate this process and make coordination easier. Evgeny Morozov has written about the technological possibilities of today's 'feedback infrastructure', which make it possible to bring different parties together to help distribute information about economic needs through non-market forms of social coordination.[43] Responding to Hayek's theory about markets as the best discovery mechanism, Morozov proposes a form of 'solidarity as a discovery mechanism' through the design of new social institutions that could coordinate economic activity more effectively than the market. Digital platforms make it easier than ever before to examine new ways of distributing resources through democratic methods.

SOCIALIST PLURALISM

Within the broad framework of different forms of social ownership, participatory planning and a collaborative culture, there is no single model of economic organisation that needs to dominate. A genuinely emancipatory economy with democratic control over investment, worker-owned firms and other forms of co-operative associations would not need to completely abolish private property or markets. Developing an economy that avoids the centralising impulse towards one single mode of economic life would create an open and diverse set of relations in which people found different ways to satisfy their needs in a mixed economy. Just as there can be many market economies, so too can there be different kinds of mixed economies. The ones we are used to in Europe in the postwar period were predominantly based on private ownership with a limited role for state regulation and public enterprise.[44] This priority needs to be reversed so that collaboration rather than competition (and the pursuit for the common good rather than selfish private interest) become the hegemonic forms of economic rationality.

Cole and Neurath both shared this commitment to economic pluralism in how they conceived of a future socialist society. For Cole,

> The very last thing I want, in working for Socialism, is to impose on society a flat uniformity of organisation or opinion. I want a social system which, taking as its basis the inescapable hugeness of modern productive technique, will nevertheless find room and opportunity for individuals to express themselves, and to serve the community in many and diverse ways.[45]

Neurath was also critical of conceptions of socialism that were intolerant towards different traditions, particularly those that did not originate with the modern industrial proletariat: 'Community economy, guild economy, social economy characterise certain periods, but they also exist side by side and give satisfaction to different types of human being.'[46] He recognised that there were a number of older traditions of mutualism and cooperation that could not simply be dismissed as conservative relics of the past.

This commitment to diversity also extends to how such cooperative practices could be taken up in different cultures and national contexts. Unlike the universalising imperative of the nation state system and free market economies, Cole and Neurath saw many different ways in which social ownership and collective control could be exercised. Neurath noted that, 'if socialism should bring liberation, it must be joined by tolerance, it must do justice to the differences in civilisations and fit each one into the economic plan and the administrative economy in its own way.'[47] The global struggle against capitalist neoliberalism could take many different forms and be understood and interpreted differently through diverse cultures and traditions.

There are serious limitations we face in discussing different economic models, particularly when hypothesising about as yet untried systems that may lead to unforeseen issues arising through their implementation. The point of the above discussion has not been to propose one specific model but to chart a direction of travel for new ways to organise economic decision-making. Problems of complexity, scale and how different social conditions will lead to different types of behaviour make it difficult to prescribe in advance the minute details of a complete alternative to capitalism. We have sufficient insight as to the current problems of our economic system to propose possible starting points, but the precise structure of a new system – and its exact configuration of market and non-market forms of social coordination – remains an issue requiring much further elaboration as conditions develop.

Much has changed since the industrial democracy of the early twentieth century, but we can take inspiration from this attempt to show what a functional democratic society could look like. As Cole himself said, 'the principles behind guild socialism are far more important than the actual forms of organisation which guild socialists have thought out'.[48] Drawing from this vision of a participatory and democratic society, the writings of Cole and Neurath assist us in developing new principles for democratic platform governance. We now move on to Chapters 6 and 7, which examine how a range of digital platforms could be democratised from the municipal to the international in the pursuit of a fairer digital economy.

6
Building Civic Platforms

Platform socialism starts at the local level with services delivered by organisations that promote inclusion, social ownership and community control. We should foster the development of broad-based ownership structures, including workers' co-operatives, community and municipal ownership and small and medium-sized private enterprises. There are two traditions that offer important intellectual resources for civic platforms at the level of the firm and the city: platform co-operativism and the 'new municipalist' movement. Each could play a key role in the political transformation towards platform socialism.

Platform co-operatives are digital platforms owned and controlled by the people who participate in them.[1] Workers have the opportunity to receive the full fruits of their labour and can take part in the governance of the business. By providing fair work to member/owners and building wealth in local communities, they offer a more ethical alternative to current corporate digital platforms. There is an emerging global movement of platform co-operativists organised around the Platform Cooperativism Consortium based at the New School for Social Research in New York City.[2] These co-operatives operate in many countries across the globe, from India and Brazil to Hong Kong and Malaysia.

We can also draw inspiration from the 'new municipalism' movement represented by cities across the world who gathered for the Fearless Cities summits.[3] This movement argues that municipality is a strategically important site for experimenting with how citizens can take back power. One of its core demands is for a decentralisation and devolution of power away from the nation state and towards local authorities who can respond better to the specific needs of their citizens. However, this is not simply a parochial 'localism' that forgoes addressing global problems and the international dimensions of corporate power. It is a transnational movement that aims to demonstrate how local issues that immediately affect citizens are connected to similar issues affecting others across the globe. New municipalists do not simply want to transfer power from one geographic location to another – they aim to transform how that power operates. The movement advocates creating a qualitative shift towards more participatory forms of self-governing community life.

Platform socialism can learn from these projects of autonomy in which devolution is combined with a broader agenda of empowering citizens and enabling them to control institutions that exercise power over their lives. At the same time, it needs to caution against falling into a localist trap of assuming that all our problems can be solved through devolving power and putting our faith in small-scale alternatives to global platforms. Case studies from these two traditions are useful because they provide working examples that show how communities could begin to organise their lives outside of the exploitation and control of corporate platforms. We need to foster these working prototypes to show that we can have efficiency *and* solidarity; innovation *and* equality. Developing alternatives from the local to the international level will ensure a rich diversity of organisational forms that are able to solve problems at different points in the system.

CULTIVATING LOCAL CO-OPERATIVE ECONOMIES

Platform co-operatives empower workers by providing them with an institutional structure of self-government and collaborative value creation. Workers' co-operatives have a long history harking back to the Rochdale Society of Equitable Pioneers, founded in 1844. They serve as an important model for collective ownership and workplace democracy. The platform co-operative movement shares an affinity with earlier models of the internet when it was an open, shared and collaborative space. The movement aims to facilitate a new kind of digital work that avoids the precarious labour and hidden forms of data capture endemic in the gig economy. It focuses on decentralising power, sharing the wealth produced in the digital economy among workers and facilitating more community involvement.

One example of such a co-operative business is Up&Go, a digital marketplace for professional home services in New York City that advertises worker-owned businesses with fair work practices. For workers undertaking a wide variety of services, from house cleaning to dog walking and handywork, the platform Up&Go allows them to keep 95 per cent of the money from jobs rather than the 50–80 per cent on other non-cooperative platforms.[4] Not only do the workers receive higher wages, they also have an ownership stake in the platform and can decide how much commission the platform takes to keep the service running.

Advocates of platform co-operativism such as Trebor Scholz – one of the key organisers of the movement – support creating a nurturing ecosystem for a co-operative economy within which individual platform co-operatives could thrive.[5] Co-operatives depend on alliances between other co-operatives, ethical sources of finance, appropriate legal and regulatory regimes and a supportive culture. The downside to all of these necessary conditions is that platform co-operatives can appear as delicate specimens, destined only to survive in a very specific and artificial environment. Faced with competitive capitalist markets, co-operatives can find it difficult to scale up and compete against existing corporate models. But despite these hurdles, there is great potential for the movement to grow and develop if it is able to navigate three fundamental dangers: losing its political mission, becoming separated from a broader institutional framework and becoming elitist and non-inclusive.

BETWEEN ENTREPRENEURSHIP AND EMANCIPATION

The first risk of platform co-operativism relates to an ambivalence regarding the precise aims of the movement and its relationship to existing economic and political structures. Are co-operatives just a better business model or do they stand for an alternative way of organising the economy? Sociologist Marisol Sandoval has highlighted the paradox of platform co-operativism's 'entrepreneurial activism': 'on the one hand it seeks to restore a collective alternative imagination, but on the other hand it surrenders to market power by relying on the organisational form of a business enterprise to advance this vision'.[6] Ed Mayo, the former secretary general of Co-operatives UK, understands the 'co-operative advantage' as its ability to offer a more competitive and sustainable business model. He argues that co-operatives are more resilient, have less staff turnover and lower absenteeism rates and can be more innovative in comparison to conventional firms.[7] In this vein, the former UK Conservative prime minister, David Cameron, described co-operatives as 'a very powerful business model and one I admire'.[8] This is not the endorsement one would expect for a transformative leftist project.

A different vision for the future of platform co-operativism that also permeates the movement is one in which worker-owned co-operatives are actively disrupting the capitalist economy and gradually replacing it with a co-operative alternative. This more radical agenda can be traced back to early co-operative thinkers such as Robert Owen and even Karl Marx who viewed workers' co-ops as 'great social experiments' that could serve as transitional institutions between a capitalist and future communist society.[9]

As Rosa Luxemburg saw, the issue with workers' co-operatives is that they are a 'hybrid form in the midst of capitalism'. In this precarious position, she argued that they 'are obliged to take toward themselves the role of capitalist entrepreneur – a contradiction that accounts for the failure of production co-operatives, which either become pure capitalist enterprises or, if the workers' interests continue to predominate, end by dissolving'.[10] Luxemburg highlighted how, if co-operatives find it difficult to compete with capitalist platforms to secure finance, they could be incentivised to engage in 'self-exploitative' practices or adopt similar practices to their competitors to survive. This is why platform co-operativism cannot lose sight of its broader political struggle against capitalism and remain content to build small co-operative islands in a sea of corporate giants. If platform co-operativism is reduced to simply a better way of doing business for members it loses its emancipatory potential.

MUNICIPAL INFRASTRUCTURE
FOR THE CO-OPERATIVE ECONOMY

Public authorities can play an important role in supporting co-operative and social enterprises in their area. Considered on their own, platform co-operatives are limited in the capital they can raise and their ability to scale. To ameliorate this, municipalities can provide public infrastructure and resources to the co-operative sector through investment and favourable procurement strategies. This could also include municipal banks radically expanding the provision of public assistance to those often denied commercial loans.

We shouldn't view 'public' infrastructure as being in fundamental opposition to the non-state, citizen-led, self-governing 'commons'. Government coordination and enforcement can often be an important institutional mechanism to secure public goods and spaces for common forms of life.[11] One example of this currently in operation is Coòpolis, a centre for co-operatives in Barcelona which promotes the social and solidarity economy in the city.[12] Its aim is to foster the development of new co-operatives and help create new jobs in existing ones.

Another striking example comes from Argentina. In May 2020, the political party Ciudad Futura (Future City) and the Social and People's Front developed Mercado Justo (Fair Market), a municipal e-commerce platform for the sale of local goods and services in Rosario, Argentina.[13] Competing directly with the Argentinian Amazon equivalent, Mercado Libre (Free Market), local authorities built Mercado Justo on the values of 'proximity, solidarity and community' with the aim of promoting local producers, strengthening economic networks and supporting co-operatives.

In London, Islington Council has supported the creation of Space4, a tech co-op working space run by digital agency Outlandish, with the aim of nurturing new start-ups in the co-operative digital economy.[14] It has also funded Wings, a new co-operative food delivery platform in the Finsbury Park area that offers living wages to riders, runs a zero emissions service and attempts to shift customers away from the exploitative model of the major food delivery platform companies.[15]

One alternative model of economic ownership that could assist digital civic platforms is public–common partnerships (PCPs), which allow local communities and municipal authorities to participate in a joint enterprise. Arising as a response to public–private partnerships, PCPs give power back to communities and allow them to have a stake in their local economy. According to this framework, outlined in a 2019 report by Keir Milburn and Bertie Russell for Common Wealth, services would be run by a joint enterprise co-owned and co-managed by a community association and a state authority.[16]

This is less a precise institutional model to be followed and more a set of guidelines for how the public can be brought back in through new forms of common ownership that avoid the pitfalls of privately run businesses seeking to make a quick buck at the public's expense. It's a plan for more decentralised democratic governance that could be developed on a case-by-case basis according to the needs and capacities of the local community. For one example of this model in practice we could turn to the German energy co-operative BEG Wolfhagen, which pays local residents an annual divided and allows them to take part in decisions of how profits from the company are invested.[17] These kinds of arrangements could be expanded to other services such as housing, domestic services and food delivery.

AGAINST 'LUXURY CO-OPERATIVISM'

The final risk for platform co-operativism emerges if it develops in an exclusionary manner that ignores the needs of the most marginalised and vulnerable. A change in ownership model is no guarantee that other forms of social power – from racism to sexism and ableism – will not continue to be reproduced within the space. Platform labour researcher Niels van Doorn has argued that the gig economy thrives off a surplus population of racialised and gendered subjects who are exploited in low-income service work.[18] Platform co-ops must be founded with a deep commitment to social justice which should be considered in all processes of institutional design and governance practices. The fear is that failing to confront these power hierarchies head on will lead to existing patterns of inequality being preserved under a new guise in co-operative enterprises. As with the Up&Go example, co-operatives can be important vehicles for marginalised communities to secure income and better employment. But, as Juliet Schor has argued,

> If you are interested in social justice, then you should know that in non-profit spaces, there are high levels of race, class, and gender exclusion. People act in ways that reinforce their own class position or their own racial position. These spaces are often more problematic from the perspective of race, class, and gender than many for-profits. So if you want to build a platform that attracts people across class, race, and gender, you need to start with the group of people that you want to attract to your platform.[19]

Platform co-operatives should be oriented to helping those workers in low-income labour markets who have suffered the most from the neoliberal revolution.

Co-operatives should also strive not to silo themselves off from broader social struggle. Once in competition with other firms, there is a tendency to pursue goals that would advance the interests of the co-operative and to become detached from social issues. The platform co-operative movement works best alongside other forms of activism and political change. This would involve working through trade unions, municipal associations and political parties.

The genuine benefits of co-operatives should not be ignored or downplayed. Workers in co-operative businesses consistently report greater satisfaction with their work and are happier and more productive. Platform co-operatives can play a vital role as one piece of a broader institutional puzzle of a new economic system. This would work best if platform co-operatives were embedded in the larger political project of platform socialism so as to better achieve their mission.

CIVIC INNOVATION

Many of the critical aspects of the platform economy, from transport to food delivery and short-term rentals, occur within the jurisdiction of city governments. The city offers a meaningful scale at which changes can occur to service delivery that directly affects citizens' lives. It is the city, rather than the nation state, which should be the priority of a movement for new forms of democratic control over digital platforms. What happens when municipalist movements meet digital technology?

'Smart cities' promise us a future in which data enables local authorities to create more equitable and sustainable lived environments. Yet the evidence of existing experiments suggests there is a gap between the rhetoric of smart city initiatives and what they have achieved in practice.[20] Big Tech has pushed for its technology to be integrated into city infrastructure because they see this as a key site for the creation of a future they seek to control. The origins of the 'smart city' framework lie in a project championed by the likes of IBM and Cisco to optimise urban infrastructure through digital sensors that provide a variety of technological solutions to urban planning problems. Jathan Sadowski has shown that this movement has been underpinned by an ideology of importing entrepreneurialism into town halls to enable corporations to monetise urban spaces.[21]

It may be that this wave of enthusiasm for smart cities has begun to dwindle. Following a peak of 30 active projects in 2015, only one of the top five suppliers deployed any smart city technology in 2020.[22] Citizens are also increasingly concerned about surveillance and manipulation from tech companies who see the idea of smart cities as a way to integrate their products into nearly every dimension of urban life. The Alphabet spinoff, Sidewalk Labs, cancelled plans to transform the Toronto waterfront into a tech-driven urban environment after protests from residents and concerns from regulators around data collection and digital governance.[23]

However, there are examples demonstrating how cities can flip the script of the traditional smart city model and show how technology can work for citizens. Since being named European Capital of Innovation in 2014, Barcelona has developed over a hundred projects on Urban Platform, which hosts projects such as ubiquitous public wifi, upgraded traffic lights, telecare services and shared electric cars.[24] Since the election of a new mayor in 2015, the citizen platform, Barcelona en Comú (Barcelona in Common) has implemented new bottom-up forms of democratic participation that put people first in how technology is used. They have shown that technology in itself does not automatically produce egalitarian outcomes – these have to be consciously designed into projects.

This shift in priorities began with a new collaborative platform, Decidim, to create the government's agenda based on citizen proposals.[25] This new form of citizen participation into government strategic planning enabled the mayor to focus on issues that people care about, such as affordable housing, healthcare, sustainability, mobility, fighting climate change and creating more green spaces. By starting with the social and environmental challenges and then seeing how technology could be employed to solve these, the model shows how data infrastructure can be used to serve the agenda of the people rather than technology companies.

The city also participated in DECODE (Decentralised Citizen-Owned Data Ecosystems), a series of pilot studies in Barcelona and Amsterdam between 2017 and 2019 that trialled new technology which put people in control of their personal data.[26] In one of the pilot projects, the city gave residents sensors to place in their neighbourhoods which were integrated into the city's sensor network gathering data on air quality, energy usage and noise pollution. The project allowed for anonymised data sharing to create public value from a data commons. The digital architecture of the platform established a new system of decentralised data governance and identity management that protected citizens' privacy and allowed them to decide what data they wanted to keep private and what they felt comfortable sharing. The pilot demonstrated the efficacy of a system of privacy-enhanced data sharing to create public value.

These pioneering innovations are paving the way for new ways of thinking about collaborative uses of digital infrastructure and data. Public platforms operated by municipal authorities are a key pillar of this new agenda. Cities are an important site for new prototypes to be developed because they are responsible for running basic services like transportation, sanitation and the maintenance of public spaces. They can also be amenable to transformative projects that improve the lives of citizens. Experiments like DECODE have shown in practice that a different institutional configuration of digital infrastructure, public policy and citizen participation is possible and affordable.[27] The democratic control over digital infrastructure works and is ready to be scaled through greater investment in a digital future that is sustainable and democratic.

It is also worth noting that decentralisation would not necessarily involve the proliferation of hundreds of different incompatible platforms. Currently, the main obstacle to cross-platform compatibility has been tech giants consciously designing barriers for interoperability into their products. If every city had their own municipal ride hail platform, for example, the software could be cloned so that signing into the app in different cities would automatically update to the specific rules and features of that city's services. Alternative platforms such as Fairbnb. coop, a platform co-op in the short-term rental market, have begun experimenting with allowing a community of hosts to have more control over the rules of the platform in their city.[28]

BUILDING A DATA COMMONS

A reliance on private companies to provide the infrastructure of projects has led to a lack of control over how data is collected and handled. Companies currently use data collected through digital platforms as a commodity to generate economic value for shareholders. Data ends up being siloed and controlled by a few individuals with little benefit flowing to citizens. Due to the way it has been abused by these companies, the very idea of data collection has developed sinister connotations of surveillance and manipulation. When platforms do produce reports they often involve the highly questionable and selective use of data to promote the company and shine a positive light on its activities.[29] We need a new way of thinking about data not as a commodity to be further protected by stronger intellectual property laws but as a collective resource that could be used to empower citizens and provide them with tools to tackle their own problems.

A data commons could be based on other commons models like free and open software, Creative Commons and Wikipedia in which a community collectively governs the use of the resource through democratic participation.[30] Rather than conceiving of data primarily as the personal property of an individual, the creation of communal rights to data can help unlock its relational value when aggregated and processed in large volumes. Considered in this way, data can be part of broader public infrastructure alongside other digital and communications services. It has huge potential to help deliver significant public benefits and solve pressing problems around transport, housing, health services and the environment. There are promising signs that people would be open to greater use of data by trusted authorities for the explicit purpose of creating public value. Polls have shown that 73 per cent of citizens in the UK are willing to share certain aspects of their data with research organisations if it can be shown to benefit themselves and others.[31]

There is no single model of how a data commons should be organised. Each institution would need to be designed based on the needs of the community, the type of data and how it could be collected and used. These would range from large-scale public data trusts (for health, science and mobility) to commercial and financial data firms and local data co-operatives.[32] The idea of a data commons allows people to share their data in a rights-preserving manner that doesn't strip individuals of their personal autonomy. It ensures that citizens can establish the level of anonymity they desire and allows them not to be identified without their consent. In this way, it provides options for citizens to choose what kinds of information to share and with whom.

A key benefit of a data commons is the enhanced control it offers communities over their own data, enabling them to decide on shared rules for how the communal resources will be used. The creation of communal rights to the data also emphasises that it is the public who should be the main beneficiary of the value derived from their data. While private companies keep their data collection and use as a trade secret, a data commons would encourage participation and debate over the public use of technology. In the DECODE pilots, increased citizen engagement opened conversations between citizens and civic authorities about how data was used in the city.

One tension of a data commons is the balance between the potential benefits of large shared troves of data versus the harm that could be caused from their misuse. Data collection and use must be consensual, fair and transparent. In some cases, certain types of data simply shouldn't be collected because the risk posed to individuals is too high. No security system is fail-safe and we should think carefully before collecting any type of data and ask first whether it is necessary and potentially of public value. There are other forms of discriminatory data gathering which should be eliminated outright. This includes carceral technology to assist predictive policing, which Ruha Benjamin in *Race after Technology* has called to be abolished.[33]

For data that is collected, individuals should have the right to anonymity and to withdraw their data if they desire. They should also be able to easily understand how their data is used and for what purposes. To protect individuals, data can be shared in anonymous and privacy-protecting ways using new decentralised tools such as distributed ledger technology. This allows computations to be performed by a distributed network of computers without a single actor owning and controlling all of the data. Transactions on the ledger can be checked without disclosing the personal information of users. In one of the DECODE pilots, all operations were processed on a distributed ledger called Chainspace, which protected the privacy of participants.[34] Security and privacy concerns are still big issues that will need further work, but existing projects have demonstrated viable prototypes.

Cities can also make ethics and security by design as the norm for how municipal authorities and businesses run services at the city level. Data commons can be developed in municipalities through public procurement that writes data sovereignty clauses into contracts with other organisations. Barcelona City Council, for example, has forced Vodafone, the city's telecom service provider, to hand over the data it collects from the public, which is now published on the council's open data portal.[35] This helps challenge the de facto position of private companies that they are entitled to commercially exploit any data they can capture from their platforms. Ownership over data can often be a murky grey area because there can be multiple parties involved who may feel they have proprietary interests in the data. A presumption in favour of open data should replace the current attempt by tech companies to gain exclusive possession. Releasing open datasets would also allow others to build on them and develop new tools, policies and actions that could benefit the public.

A data commons has a huge potential to create a launching pad for further innovation and development. It provides enormous public benefit while at the same time putting citizens in control of their digital future. Barcelona offers one innovative example of redefining smart cities, but there are possibilities of going further still in designing new democratic platforms that benefit the people who use them. There are a number of services that would make more sense if they were undertaken by public authorities and integrated into other service provisions. Two promising examples are ride hail platforms and short-term rental services.

RIDE HAIL PLATFORMS

The first example is the possibility of a municipally owned and operated on-demand ride hail platform. London provides an important test case because it is a densely populated and highly connected city, and it is one of the few cities in which Uber currently turns a profit. A municipally owned platform in this city could be called RideLondon, following the example of GoSutton, a twelve-month trial of an on-demand bus service that allowed customers to request a ride through an app and select their pick-up and drop-off points within the Outer London borough of Sutton.[36] RideLondon would be administered by Transport for London (TfL), an existing government body that runs London's efficient public transport system.

This municipal service would replace corporate ride hail platforms, which would not be granted a licence to compete against the publicly operated system. The service wouldn't face the problem of a lack of access to capital due to its incorporation within TfL, an organisation with an annual budget of £9.7 billion.[37] Using existing knowledge of the network and data from current transportation systems, TfL is ideally placed to create an integrated system with an on-demand service that is able to complement rather than compete with existing public transport options.

The board of RideLondon should include appointments selected by municipal authorities, workers and commuters. Workers on the service would have a special interest in how their daily working life was organised and should have a priority say over this aspect of the labour process. Drivers should be able to determine the conditions of their work, how service delivery and rota systems are organised, which incentive structures are in place and other aspects of how the technology intersects with their work environment. The service could also be opened up to participation and co-governance from commuters by creating forums for new initiatives to be proposed and the priorities of the organisation to be voted upon by the people who use the service.

Such a system would provide several important advantages, starting with combating increased congestion and pollution. A recent study by Transport & Environment found a 23 per cent increase in overall CO_2

emissions from the private vehicle hire sector since Uber arrived in London.[38] This amounts to an extra 250,000 cars on the road or half a megaton of CO_2. While the underlying mission of private operators is to increase use of their platform, a municipal service could fill the gap of an on-demand service while at the same time nudging users towards more efficient public transport options. A successful socially owned platform would be one that reduced demand by connecting customers to more environmentally friendly alternatives.

It would also be able to match Uber's powerful network effects because its data-gathering capacity would mean similar positive feedback loops in which an increase in one area would favourably impact other areas: from increased demand to more drivers, more data, faster pick-up times and greater brand recognition. TfL could advertise its service through its own network and encourage existing public transport users to download its app. Profits gained from the service could also subsidise travel for people with disabilities or health problems such as TfL's existing service, London Dial-a-Ride for commuters unable to use public transport.[39]

The design of the software and functionality of the platform would also need to be redesigned with workers' interests at its core. Rather than relying on a 'gamification' designed to keep drivers on the road for as long as possible, the platform would prioritise the physical and mental health of workers.

A fairer alternative might be theoretically possible, but would people use it? A study commissioned by the New Economics Foundation found that 82 per cent of Uber customers would be willing to use a more ethical alternative and that 54 per cent would pay more for their journey if drivers were given better pay and conditions.[40]

Several on-demand services are currently being trialled in London and results from these will dictate whether more ambitious proposals would ever be considered. In the meantime, black cab drivers have developed their own platform, TaxiApp, which is owned and operated by the drivers, providing fair pay and challenging Uber's aggressive pricing structure.[41]

A municipally owned service might not be feasible in certain other cities that are too small or with insufficiently developed public transport infrastructure. In these cases, worker-owned platform co-operatives also offer a viable alternative to exploitative platform companies. Non-profits have operated ride hail systems in cities such as Austin, Texas, which Uber and Lyft left in 2016 due to new regulations, leaving their driver 'partners' jobless with no notice.[42] In place of Uber and Lyft's opaque split system of payments, RideAustin, one of the non-profits which filled the gap, took a small fee to cover overheads with the rest of the fare going directly to drivers. In the four years of its operation, RideAustin took three million rides, paid drivers US$38 million in wages and helped raise US$450,000 for local non-profits.[43]

Uber and Lyft successfully lobbied the state government to overturn the city's regulations enabling the companies to come back into the Austin market. RideAustin experienced a 55 per cent drop in the first week from 59,000 to 26,000 rides, with the non-profit eventually closing its doors in 2020.[44] Other cities and states should take the lead on setting the agenda for how they want their ride hail services to be delivered and use procurement strategies to prioritise suppliers who will adhere to local laws, offer fair work and support the local community.

SHORT-TERM RENTAL SERVICES

In the case of housing, short-term rentals could be managed as part of a broader housing organisation which balanced the needs of different members of the community. The priority would be to ensure that everyone had access to secure and affordable long-term housing while allowing for flexibility in renting out rooms and some houses for vacation rentals. The organisation itself would be internally democratic and enable different stakeholders to have input into the design and management of the service. If organised at the municipal level, local councils would have the authority to create rules for their boroughs and set out the conditions under which rooms and houses could be rented for short durations. Hosts who used the service should also be able to determine priorities in how regulations are designed, but these need to be checked against the effect of these rentals on the local community.

This provides the starting point for what Janelle Orsi has called 'Munibnb' – a municipally owned platform that could be developed between several large cities to manage short-term accommodation services offered by local residents.[45] This could be a new way of structuring a broader city-managed commons – one that could effectively tax and regulate the use of property to ensure money stays within the city and benefits its residents equally.

The great advantage of control by a municipal authority is that (depending on the jurisdiction) they will sometimes have the regulatory power to ban competitor platforms and insist on maintaining high standards and a fair service for users.

A municipal authority in charge of the platform would also assist with the coordination of other housing services offered by many cities and enable action to be taken on issues of housing affordability and gentrification. They could also encourage users away from renting out entire houses on the short-term property market through increased taxes on such a service, which would alleviate housing shortages.

Switzerland's innovative housing co-operatives offer guidance for what could be the beginning of an alternative approach.[46] Housing co-operatives provide 5 per cent of the country's entire housing needs and range from small dwellings to huge complexes with over a thousand apartments. Housing projects often consist of a mixture of low- and middle-income housing with some including temporary accommodation for short-term rentals that are managed by the housing co-operative. This system offers rent that is considerably cheaper to long-term residents, with reductions up to 40 per cent of the market value for low-cost rental apartments. Short-term rentals could also be supplied to the market through the construction of housing co-operatives with temporary accommodation built into complexes to be managed by the co-operative. Visitors would then have the opportunity of visiting a new city and experiencing it as part of a larger co-operative housing ecosystem. These services would still require strict regulation at a municipal level to ensure appropriate standards were being met and residents still had access to sufficient housing stock.

REGIONAL AND NATIONAL PLATFORMS

City-wide services should not be the limit of our vision of a democratic platform economy – the national and international levels are also important spheres of reform. In countries with smaller populations and limited territory, it could be more efficient to administer services undertaken elsewhere by the city government at the regional or national level, particularly for services that require significant institutional investment.

The Covid-19 pandemic has given rise to a number of calls to nationalise various systems that offer essential services to people.[47] One prominent example has been the logistics services that have been vital to ensuring people who are shielding receive necessary supplies. In Brazil, several public platforms have been developed in response to the crisis, such as the delivery platform FiqueNoLar, which offers delivery services in the north of the country where many private delivery apps did not operate.[48] In October 2020, the Argentinian national postal service announced the creation of a state-owned online marketplace platform called Correo Compras, which offers low-cost listings for businesses and uses postal workers to carry out fulfilment.[49] Another direct competitor with the Latin American giant Mercado Libre, this 'state-owned Amazon' offers living wages to its employees and shifts away from the profit-driven model of taking a large cut from every transaction. It began by offering 2,000 products with plans to allow small and medium-sized enterprises to offer many more as it tilts the scale in favour of consumers and smaller businesses. But to have control over the digital infrastructure that powers these platforms, we should look to the infrastructure on which it runs such as the cloud services providers.

SOCIALIST CLOUD COMPUTING

Amazon Web Services is one of the most profitable parts of the Amazon empire, with the company controlling 32 per cent of the US$150 billion cloud market.[50] It requires large amounts of capital investment in data centres that host and process data for other companies and organisations. Cloud services reveal the limitations of purely bottom-up models of decentralised local initiatives. Large data centres that host and process data could not be owned and operated by small-scale community groups. This is where the connection between the local governance of small organisations needs to be combined with large-scale investment at a national level in public cloud services. A publicly owned and run cloud platform would empower decentralised groups to build their own digital tools and services on the platform. It could provide flexible on-demand use for different groups, allowing them storage and computational power to be used when necessary. This could also be combined with education programmes to open up access to these platforms to new groups of citizens who wouldn't have otherwise had the knowledge to use them.

We should also look to break up the power of large cloud computing companies by building more decentralised networking that could be used alongside them. One example is the FreedomBox project launched in 2010 by legal scholar Eben Moglen and colleagues, which provides the hardware for a grassroots community model of server provision.[51] The device can be plugged into the wall and operates as a local cloud with a wireless access point and a hard drive for data storage. It can enable Tor, routing users' traffic through the Tor network to provide them with anonymity in addition to other in-built security and privacy features. The FreedomBox bypasses the need for intermediary web services like Amazon Web Services and provides a secure means of engaging in online activities for a local neighbourhood by providing 'out of the box' privacy guarantees and encrypted communication services.

Public cloud computing would also provide an opportunity for national governments to offer more of their administrative services on government platforms. Estonia's e-Estonia project is a pioneering example of a comprehensive programme of digital government that provides citizens with an e-Identity and e-Services portal.[52] Its data storage and management systems are also examples of how public services could provide security for citizens' data. After gaining independence from the Soviet Union in 1991, Estonia was not encumbered by longstanding systems of public administration and was able to invest in building a digital infrastructure for twenty-first-century government, assisted by the Open Estonia Foundation. As a result, most Estonians can now access 99 per cent of government services online and can fill in their tax return online in a matter of minutes.

But this raises many concerns about possible security breaches and the abuse of citizens' data. For example, Estonia's digital government was targeted by Russian hackers in 2007 who took down 58 of Estonia's websites including those of the government, most newspapers and many banks.[53] As a result of this attack, Estonia has researched new techniques for maintaining the security of its public systems. It has invested in extra security in the Estonian Government Cloud, a platform that delivers IT services to the government sector.[54] It has also developed the first example of a data embassy by signing an agreement with Luxembourg in 2017 allowing Estonian public records to be stored in a secure location outside the country – while still legally under Estonian jurisdiction – to ensure digital continuity in the case of cyber attacks.[55] The data embassy currently acts as a backup and provides additional computing power for datasets considered critical for the functioning of the state.

Nextcloud Hub is another example of an integrated on-premises content collaboration platform that a number of EU governments are adopting to provide them with independence from private US cloud services.[56] This offers government agencies digital tools and storage, which protects their digital sovereignty and provides them with control over their own data. It might also be possible for several national governments to share access to a public cloud service, enabling states that cannot afford them to still use them or to jointly fund and administer a regional service.

Modelled on the e-Estonia project and the DECODE pilot at a city level, citizens could have their personal information stored in a secure digital wallet in a public cloud. This information would have data related to their demographic information, health records, employment records and mobility data. It would be stored with mechanisms to empower citizens to decide how and on what terms they wanted to make this information accessible to researchers, civil servants or various tiers of government to provide better services. Promoting anonymised data sharing at a national and international level can also help create open and shared services that could be used by business, non-profits and government across the world. When organisations wanted to use the data they would do so in a heavily regulated environment in which they would have to respect privacy restrictions.

The guiding question of this chapter has been: how do we maximise the level of democratic participation and control over systems with a natural tendency towards oligarchy and the centralisation of power? What I have tried to emphasise is that there isn't a straightforward technological solution that doesn't directly confront questions of power and politics.

7
Global Digital Services

The most challenging aspect of the creation of a democratic digital economy is the need for action at the international level to combat the vast inequalities that exist between different countries and to coordinate alternatives on a global scale. As we move from the local to the global, the enormity of the challenge becomes more evident. It is not enough to carve out small pockets of resistance at the margins of global capitalism or for experiments to remain as local co-operatives serving only a handful of people.

Large platform companies are global in their ambitions. Platform companies use their knowledge as long-term players to fight regulations across multiple jurisdictions and employ their subsidiary companies to evade taxation and legal challenges. If we want to avoid ceding the future to these private empires then our vision of a democratic digital economy has to be international in scope.

Movements towards an alternative global system may seem improbable in today's climate. The most radical ideas currently receiving mainstream support are limited to anti-monopoly sentiments and tougher regulations on Big Tech's use of data. But things could change very quickly, and when they do we need to be ready with a vision for our democratic digital future.

The future of digital platforms and the development of new technology is increasingly tied to a global struggle between the US and China. Leading figures in the US tech industry are pushing for 'hundreds of billions in federal spending in the coming years' based on fears that China is closing in on the US in the development of AI and quantum computing.[1] The United States National Security Commission on Artificial Intelligence, which includes senior executives from Microsoft, Google, Amazon and Oracle, warned that the US may lose its leadership position to China within the next decade, stoking fears of a new digital cold war between the two superpowers.

Between China's authoritarian state-led technological ambitions and the United States' free market 'industry self-regulation' approach, there is space for a non-aligned movement of countries to promote a democratic alternative for AI and digital platforms. Europe shows more promising signs of pursuing a 'third way' focusing on digital sovereignty, regulating the use of AI and boosting local digital industry. Europe is a relatively small player in terms of investment in technology, but it sees itself as a world leader in developing new regulatory approaches that protect privacy, competition and safe data practices.

A transnational solidarity movement could prevent multinational companies from completely shaping the agenda and entrenching US and Chinese hegemony. International cooperation is needed around developing local technology that is participatory, public interest-oriented and designed to serve citizens' basic needs. Such a coalition would face three primary challenges moving forward: combating global inequalities, pooling investment and coordinating open and democratic alternatives. First, we need to actively fight against the inequalities and neocolonial relations that are currently built into the global system. We do not want rich countries with highly developed and generous public digital systems while countries in the Global South are still exploited by private companies. Second, a global movement for a democratic digital future would require large investments from multiple states, including resources for creating new infrastructure, scaling up existing prototypes and investing in new research and development. Third, we need an international movement for cooperation across borders to build new code and software through a free and open-source software movement.

This chapter explores new institutional arrangements around democratic ownership and governance for the digital economy with the goal of creating a diverse ecosystem of platforms. The economic benefits of these tools should be shared more widely and the political structure and decision-making over how these services are run should be opened to community participation. This requires moving beyond the regulatory and market-driven approaches that have dominated in policy circles and thinking about genuine alternatives.

DIGITAL COLONIALISM

The tech industry is a leading player in new forms of digital colonialism. Control over the digital ecosystem – including hardware, software and network connectivity – gives direct power to US (and increasingly Chinese) multinational tech firms who use it to extract rent, gather valuable datasets and extend their hegemony over how technology develops across the globe. Michael Kwet has argued that just as the railways and maritime trade routes provided the 'open veins' of classic colonialism, the digital infrastructure and proprietary services of the Big Tech firms now play a similar role in the plunder of the Global South.[2] Just as before, this infrastructure is designed to extract value from target countries under the purportedly benevolent goal of 'connecting the world'. Establishing their infrastructure and services as the default helps firms prevent other countries developing their own alternatives to Big Tech's products, thus keeping populations in the Global South in a position of permanent dependency. Big Tech also cooperates with US national intelligence organisations as part of a global surveillance system that violates users' privacy and hands over data to state agencies.

Big Tech CEOs act as envoys, meeting heads of state and offering shiny deals of free infrastructure and services in exchange for the collection of data and control over the system. This includes cloud services to government agencies, building broadband cables and even using high-altitude balloons to create an aerial wireless network connecting remote areas of the country.[3] Facebook's notorious 'Free Basics' offers a bare-bones version of the internet to countries in the Global South who receive free access to a limited number of data-light websites and services. Facebook had to cancel the programme in India because of protests that it embedded Facebook's gatekeeper role and limited people's experience of the internet to the world of the big platforms.

Big Tech is also trying to solidify its position by investing in software in Global South classrooms to entice young people into using its products form an early age. US companies have subsidised tech equipment and software in the hope of forging path dependencies and shaping the habits of the next generation of users from childhood. This also privatises public education infrastructure and enables tech companies to gain valuable data produced by students to develop new services.

This system of digital colonialism is also in the process of being entrenched at the level of international law and trade agreements. Since 2017, more than 70 countries, including the US and China, have been in negotiations in the World Trade Organisation for a new treaty on e-commerce.[4] Big Tech companies are looking to solidify their dominance by sponsoring a new framework for keeping data flows as unrestricted as possible and maintaining their position as market leaders. If these companies succeed in establishing a new global agreement it could help entrench their position for decades to come.

A GLOBAL DIGITAL SERVICES ORGANISATION

To prevent Big Tech from furthering its own agenda through a new legal framework, we need more international coordination against the agenda of digital colonialism. The Global Digital Services Organisation (GDSO) could be established as an autonomous organisation working with the United Nations as a specialised agency alongside the International Telecommunications Union and the International Labour Organization. It could be founded through a levy on global profits of tech companies and would receive ongoing funding from member states' contributions to the UN.

The aim of the GDSO would be to improve people's access to digital communications technology by developing and supporting essential digital services for people to connect online. This would include championing fast and free broadband access as a universal right and funding projects to expand internet connectivity, particularly in countries in the Global South. It would also involve funding developers to create a diverse ecosystem of digital platforms so that we have a range of well-designed and user-friendly software that operates on common protocols and standards.

The organisation would also act as an advocacy body, raising awareness of inequalities in access to digital services, misinformation and censorship. It would play an active role in setting international standards for digital services and supporting new initiatives and campaigns in the field. The organisation would hold forums and encourage debate about how current digital services could be redesigned to better serve citizens' needs. This would build on important work undertaken by digital rights groups such as the Web Foundation, the Electronic Frontiers Foundation and many others in advancing a vision of the web as a public good and a basic right.

Membership of the GDSO would be open to all member states of the United Nations. The GDSO would hold a conference once a year to set broad policies, elect an executive body and appoint key technical experts. Each member state would be entitled to be represented by a delegation consisting of one government-appointed representative, one representative from civil society and one member of the public selected by lot. All delegates would have the same rights, could express themselves freely and vote as they like. Heads of state and government ministers could attend as observers.

Each member state should also organise their own Digital Citizens' Assembly: a national assembly of citizens selected by lot from a pool of volunteers on a yearly rotating basis. These assemblies could be organised through the digital and democratic platform, Decidim – software trialled in Barcelona that enables citizen participation in decision-making. The assemblies would be spaces for citizens to launch citizen initiatives, debate proposals put forward by other assemblies and vote on what they wanted the organisation to do. These public deliberations would also enable greater scrutiny and oversight of the day-to-day running of the organisation. The executive body would be bound to act upon decisions approved by a majority of assemblies. This would open up a space for the global community to exercise meaningful power to determine the shape and mission of the organisation and exercise direct influence over representatives.

Of the many activities the organisation could support, this chapter explores three specific initiatives in more detail: establishing a Global Digital Wealth Fund, developing a public internet search engine and supporting a federal and distributed network of non-proprietary social media platforms.

ESTABLISHING A GLOBAL DIGITAL WEALTH FUND

Many states are now making substantial investments in their long-term development of digital technology. The Chinese government has invested US$130 billion in their goal to be the world leader in AI by 2030. Japan's Vision Fund has over US$100 billion in technology-focused venture capital, which is supported by Saudi Arabia and sovereign wealth funds from several other Middle Eastern countries. A number of European countries have announced large investment programmes in technology and innovation, with France and Italy creating public venture capital funds to support private businesses and new start-ups. The question is, how can we invest in public interest technology that is decentralised and builds a democratic platform economy?

We need to establish a Global Digital Wealth Fund as a special-purpose investment fund managed by the GDSO in a fiduciary capacity on behalf of current global citizens and future generations. The fund could be based on existing sovereign and citizens' wealth funds such as the Norwegian Government Pension Fund and the Alaska Permanent Fund, which were both established from revenue generated by oil and gas fields. Rather than paying a social dividend to every citizen, the fund should be used to invest in new digital infrastructure and help finance socially beneficial campaigns and programmes established by the GDSO.

The GDSO would vote on a constitution of basic principles to govern the use of the fund which would then be put to a vote of the Digital Citizens' Assemblies. The fund would be managed by an independent commission appointed by the GDSO who would oversee the development projects in which it invested. It would require expert managers to help grow the fund but also democratic oversight to ensure that it was being spent on ethical projects in the best interest of beneficiaries.

One of the most pressing tasks would be to help connect parts of the Global South that currently lack digital services and increasing connectivity for marginalised communities in the Global North. Universal access to high-speed broadband needs to be part of any progressive reform agenda for a digital economy. The coronavirus exposed existing fault lines in the digital divide like never before, highlighting the problem that in developing countries only 47 per cent of households have an internet connection.[5] Even in the Global North, 6 per cent of the population in the US and 13 per cent in Australia have no high-speed internet connection.

Free fast-speed internet would improve public participation in civic affairs, boost productivity, reduce commuting trips, bridge the digital divide and create a more inclusive and connected society. Allowing this vital infrastructure to be left in the hands of private operators has increased inequalities and led to a rural–urban connectivity divide. A universal service would increase regional access and not suffer from the same market failures involved with companies attempting to connect people only where it is profitable for them to do so. Achieving digital equality through fast and reliable access to the internet is an essential part of a political project to achieve a more just digital economy.

BEYOND BING: DEVELOPING A PUBLIC SEARCH ENGINE

Internet search engines perform the important task of enabling anyone with an internet connection to access information on demand. Google's command of 92 per cent of the search engine market gives it a dominant position with gatekeeper power over access to the open internet. The name Google has become synonymous for search, with its closest rival, Microsoft's Bing, accounting for only 2.3 per cent of overall searches.

There are alternatives, but they remain limited both in terms of technical capacity and offering a genuine alternative to Google's advertising model. Ecosia is powered by 100 per cent renewable energy and plants trees for every search you do, but it runs on the algorithms of Microsoft's Bing. DuckDuckGo is another possibility that doesn't track you or collect information based on your previous searches. However, it is still a private company that runs on an advertising model, just without the additional information gained from tracking your activities on the web through millions of third-party sites and apps.

Access to humanity's collective knowledge should not be controlled by a profit-driven company. People should have universal and free access to all knowledge and the ability to search the web without being tracked and surveilled for advertising revenue. We need a publicly funded Google that eliminates the advertising model and enables the organisation to run an efficient search engine free at the point of use.

With some digital platforms, the question of how to transform them into infrastructure that serves the public interest is difficult because many of the exploitative practices of the company are built into the design of the business and its software. But with Google Search it is relatively straightforward to distinguish the socially useful component of the business (which enables people to search the world's information) from the advertising model that tracks users and sells insights to third parties.

One possibility would be for a group of countries to sponsor the creation of a new search tool based on the principles of a free and open internet. They would set up a foundation and pay for the data centres and engineers to create a new search engine that was funded through state donations. But even if such a tool could be created, user adoption would be an enormous problem due to Google's hegemonic position in this space. It would be likely that news of its creation would soon dissipate and it would join the collection of over 20 other search engines with less than 1 per cent of the market. This would be a significant hurdle for any kind of alternative – public or private – to Google's dominance.

A more confrontational – but potentially productive – approach would be to convert Google into a not-for-profit foundation, expropriating its assets and adapting its organisational structure to be used for the common good. This strategy would involve the transfer of capital ownership to an independent, non-partisan foundation that would be administered by the GDSO as part of its mission of providing digital services to the world. It would be achieved after a period of protracted political struggle and the formulation of the demand that access to information is too important and valuable to be left in the hands of a for-profit company.

This requisition of Google would enable the new foundation to take with it most of Google's current infrastructure, staff and software – and for users' experience of the Search function to remain relatively unchanged. Some users and staff would turn to alternative services, for ideological and practical reasons, but this wouldn't disrupt the main purpose of the foundation. We could expect that many software engineers would be glad to no longer have to work on how to optimise advertising results, and could instead focus all their energies on optimising the service and creating tools for humanity. Most millennials and generation Zs now want to work for a company with a social mission and this would allow them to do it in reality rather than just appearance.

In some respects, Google's organisation and mission might begin to look a lot more like Wikipedia. It would be a public good that embodied the ideals of equality, open access and transparency. It would also be available for all to use free of charge. Much like Wikipedia, once it was established people would wonder why we ever allowed companies to privatise access to the world's information. But there are many differences between the two services and additional challenges that a public search engine would have to face.

First, a public search engine could never be funded by the donations model of Wikipedia. Much of the labour on Wikipedia is undertaken by several hundred thousand volunteer editors who cooperate in writing and editing articles. As a result, the Wikimedia Foundation had only US$112 million in expenses in 2020. It's doubtful that a public search engine could rely on volunteer labour to the same extent as Wikipedia. The technical skills of operating an internet search engine require the employment of paid professionals to administer the service. Even a few seconds of outage of the service would have enormous consequences for the global economy.

It would also require billions of dollars of investment in data centres and infrastructure compared to the relatively small website-hosting fees of Wikipedia. When you search Google, you are not actually searching the internet but Google's index created by crawling websites, analysing the content of pages and cataloguing them in Google's database. The cost of the storage and computational capacities for constantly running this service is immense. Alphabet's annual operating expenses for 2020 were US$141.30 billion, a figure which has been steadily rising due to the increased need for more data centres and R&D. Even with the closure of the entire advertising component of the company (and not taking into consideration Google's many other projects), it would still require large and ongoing capital investment to operate the search service without being subsidised by advertising. The biggest challenge would be generating the political will to have public organisations fund a foundation to run the service on behalf of humanity.

TRANSFORMING SEARCH

What changes would need to be implemented to ensure that a non-commercial search engine operated in the public interest? Removing the advertising component of Google Search would better enable it to achieve its stated purpose, namely 'to organize the world's information and make it universally accessible and useful'. The first change would be related to transparency: Google's proprietary computer algorithms should be open, accessible and subject to political debate and public oversight. Currently, the precise ranking formula is a closely guarded secret. One of Google's algorithms, PageRank, preferences websites in terms of the number of quality links to a page and how well connected it is to other hubs and authorities. But the opacity of the company's software means we cannot be sure how one of the most important tools for accessing information actually works.

Search engine technology is not neutral but embeds certain values and biases into its design. Rather than pretend these are purely technical devices over which it is possible to achieve some version of 'objective' results, we should accept their ineliminable political character and openly discuss how we want a public search engine to operate.[6] We could seek inspiration form the Value Sensitive Design movement, which draws attention to the need for a theoretically grounded approach to tech design that discloses the often hidden values laden in the design of technology.[7] A process of ranking is necessarily going to bias certain types of information and it is important that we establish institutions and processes to educate the public and debate the relative merits of different ranking methods based on their ability to advance important social values.

One issue that would remain with a public search engine is the persistence of powerful and well-resourced groups employing strategies to achieve higher rankings. Companies currently engage in search engine optimisation to improve their chances of appearing at the top of Google's results. Although advertisers' paid positions would be removed on a public search engine, this would not affect the ability of certain groups to use their superior knowledge and resources to promote what they wanted to appear in the rankings. Some of these issues could be addressed through design features and by understanding the strategies employed by groups in order to counteract their effects, but people trying to game the system would be an ongoing challenge.

Should a public search engine track users, remember their results and optimise content for their specific needs? Google currently creates and stores a record of every search made by users and draws on over 50 different signals from user location, browser type, previous searches and demographic information to help it construct 'prediction engines' to determine what users want to see. DuckDuckGo, in contrast, claims not to profile its users or personalise search results, which means in theory each user will typically receive the same search results if they type in identical queries.

It's not clear that all users would want to abandon the beneficial consequences of search engines' uncanny ability to know what we are looking for and deliver precise results. The problem is that cookies and other tracking devices are currently designed to deliver maximum levels of data to companies and remain hidden from users' experience. The design of a new search engine should prioritise users' autonomy and privacy. They should be able to quickly and simply opt in and out of a personalised service and determine the level of personalisation for the sole purpose of delivering them better results. Personalisation of search results also mitigates against the 'winner takes all' effect of delivering the same ranked results for every user. Search engines are a powerful tool for accessing the web and the creation of a public search engine represents an important part of the broader struggle for a democratic platform economy.

SEMI-PUBLIC PLATFORMS

A platform socialist programme must also reckon with how to organise the social media ecosystem more democratically so that political speech can be expressed freely without being distorted by powerful economic interests. Corporate platforms privilege viral content that can include fake news, misinformation and hate speech, but regardless of how their algorithms operate we should be concerned with the level of unchecked power currently exercised by these corporations.

Upon announcing Trump's deplatforming following the storming of the Capitol building in January 2021, Twitter CEO Jack Dorsey admitted that this decision 'sets a precedent I feel is dangerous: the power of an individual or corporation has over part of the global public conversation'.[8] What was left out of the message was that Trump had been fanning the flames of extremism and spreading misinformation to his followers for a long time. The major platforms tolerated his behaviour, which had already violated their terms and conditions, because he generated billions of interactions for them and boosted engagement on their platforms. Repressive regimes in Sri Lanka and Myanmar have also used the platforms to inflict great harm without significant repercussions. Journalist Julio López has shown the difficulties of having the Facebook and YouTube accounts of neo-Nazi groups in Argentina blocked, despite clear links to their activities and affiliations.[9] What became untenable for the companies in Trump's case was the pushback they would have received for not taking action in their most profitable market of North America.

Social media platforms such as Facebook, Twitter and Reddit are public spaces of political communication that utilise privately owned and controlled forums in which companies set the digital architecture, format and rules for communication. They could be described as *semi-public platforms* insofar as they are neither public nor private in the traditional sense of these terms. Rather, they form a new hybrid space with significant implications for politics and our freedom. Their rise needs to be contextualised as the latest step in the commodification of our political communication.

In his classic text, *The Structural Transformation of the Public Sphere*, German philosopher Jürgen Habermas described the public sphere as an imaginary community which engages in the free exchange of ideas and debate over the rules governing society.[10] In this work, he shows that in the late eighteenth century the rise of a bourgeois class led to the development of a public sphere within a number of discursive spaces such as coffee houses, salons, libraries, newspapers and publishing houses. These new institutions organised discussion among people which was separated from the church and state and in principle open to all (although in practice open mainly to wealthy men and some women).

As this sphere of free exchange developed, it also started to be corroded by the rise of a new form of media power which came to restructure and dominate it. Privately owned media companies began to control information flows and exerted influence over public opinion formation. The dominance of corporate interests in the public sphere and the distortion of political communication has been further intensified under platform capitalism. Early utopian theories of the internet thought that we were witnessing the birth of a new medium of free communication that would open unmanipulated forms of direct exchange between citizens. But over the course of the 2000s this promise dissipated as platform companies came to dominate online spaces. Facebook, Twitter and Reddit now occupy the position of the twenty-first-century coffee shop in which debate and exchange take place within a monetised sphere of data extraction and profit generation.

DO WE WANT STATE-OWNED SOCIAL MEDIA?

There have been a number of proposals put forward for publicly owned alternatives to Facebook. During Jeremy Corbyn's leadership of the British Labour Party, one key pillar of Labour's 'digital democracy' programme was an idea that the state could sponsor a British Digital Corporation. This would be a sister organisation to the British Broadcasting Corporation that would run its own social media platform funded by a tax on tech giants ensuring 'real privacy and public control over the data'.[11] In a similar spirit, the Centre for Responsible Technology in Australia has proposed using the national broadcasting network, the Australian Broadcasting Corporation (ABC), to extend its existing online capabilities to act as a national social network platform.[12] This would build on the high levels of trust that the public has for the institution and the ABC's existing community engagement strategies.

National publicly funded social networks would be an improvement over surveillance-driven models, but there are several limitations with this option.[13] The first relates to scale. National networks wouldn't allow people to remain connected with family and friends overseas and would be poor substitutes for existing global platforms. Second, even an arm's length body such as a public media corporation would have trouble maintaining the trust needed to facilitate and moderate a forum for the free expression of political opinions. The organisation would be under pressure to adhere to certain norms of civility and might end up with an overly restrictive notion of what constitutes acceptable standards of speech. The problem would be far worse in authoritarian and semi-democratic countries in which citizens would be highly unlikely to voice critical opinions of the regime on a government-sponsored platform. Third, the centralisation and conformity of a single platform is precisely what many people find disagreeable about current arrangements. To replicate this at the level of the state seems to miss the possibility of a more exciting decentralised alternative that seems implicit in the logic of social media.

To think about decommodified alternatives to corporate social media, we can turn to some of the ideas and principles that first permeated the open internet before the rise of today's global platforms.

A FREE AND OPEN WEB

From our own slightly jaded position of data breaches and election hacking scandals, it's easy to forget the utopian spirit that once pervaded the early internet and its first netizens. In the early 1990s a general sense of openness and wonder pervaded the new technology as people imagined how all of the citizen-operated bulletin board systems, multi-user dungeons and internet relay chats of this new 'electronic frontier' would develop.

Howard Rheingold is a 'veteran of virtual community-building' and his book, *The Virtual Community*, offers an insightful guide to this era.[14] Rheingold participated in a computer conferencing system called 'the Well' (the Whole Earth 'Lectronic Link), one of the oldest virtual communities in continuous operation, founded in 1985.[15] During these early days, small communities of a few dozen or hundred people accessed community bulletin boards via dial-up modems. The internet was still at a crossroads, with the possibility of moving in radically different directions. As Rheingold recounts:

> The technology that makes virtual communities possible has the potential to bring enormous leverage to ordinary citizens at relatively little cost ... But the technology will not in itself fulfill that potential; this latent technical power must be used intelligently and deliberately by an informed population. ... The odds are always good that big power and big money will find a way to control access to virtual communities; ... The Net is still out of control in fundamental ways,

but it might not stay that way for long. What we know and do now is important because it is still possible for people around the world to make sure this new sphere of vital human discourse remains open to the citizens of the planet before the political and economic big boys seize it, censor it, meter it, and sell it back to us.[16]

The underlying structure of the web upon which today's digital platforms operate is still largely based on an open and decentralised model. Applications like the world wide web, email and peer-to-peer file sharing function through shared protocols that enable users to connect without a single central storage facility or administrative bottleneck.

Early web activists fought to retain the internet as a free and open space for civic debate, the sharing of information and community building. Tim Berners-Lee, who designed and implemented the hypertext transport protocol (HTTP), founded the World Wide Web Consortium to develop universal standards for devices to communicate with each other. The idea was that the values of openness and freedom could be built into the structure of the web using shared protocols that made it harder to suppress the exchange of information. It was only when platforms like Facebook became more dominant that they stopped supporting open protocols and attempted to force users into siloed accounts so companies could control content and collect proprietary data.

Organisations like the Free Software Foundation advocate for everyone to have the right to understand, tinker with and redistribute free software that is available to all. This represents a completely different kind of production and distribution than the proprietary model of software development pushed by Bill Gates and Microsoft. The original idea of the distributed development of software and services is still evident in the logic of the internet. A number of non-commodified platforms already exist which run on free and open-source software and offer a different vision of how to organise communications technology.[17]

DISTRIBUTED SOCIAL NETWORKING

A platform socialist model of digital communication would rely on a free and open-source ecosystem of platforms that were decentralised and interoperable. It aims to empower users and give them greater autonomy and control over their online publishing and communication. Open standards and shared protocols would make it easy for users to discover and filter other users' content and communicate within a federated framework using a variety of different software. This is in line with calls for 'protocols not platforms' to dominate the internet.[18] There is a striking resemblance between the online 'fediverse' – an ensemble of federated servers used for web publishing and communications – and the kinds of organisational structures described by G. D. H. Cole and the guild socialists. The aim of both systems was to guarantee individual autonomy within a larger federal system that coordinated action without the need for the overly centralised model of the bureaucratic state or platform monopoly.

There are a number of working examples of open and federated networks already in operation. One of the most successful of these is Mastodon, a decentralised alternative to Twitter which uses an open protocol for microblogging and status updates.[19] We could also choose from other networks like diaspora*, Friendica and GNU Social, but Mastodon has been particularly popular due to its smooth interface and attention to user experience. The project was started by Eugen Rochko, a German software developer, in October 2016 and received a wave of popularity in April 2017.[20] Each node of the Mastodon federal network has its own code of conduct, privacy options and moderation policies. Users can stay within one node but can also interact with other users in different nodes as well. Many of these distributed social networking projects begin to look less like Facebook and more like Reddit's subcommunities, with different rules and norms for each group overseen by administrators and moderators of the community.

One of the biggest hurdles of federal social networking tools has been achieving the same level of functionality as large corporate networks with funds to pay for full-time professional software developers. We have not yet seen what a well-resourced project funded by a large foundation could achieve in terms of design features and user experience. Existing alternatives have found it difficult to compete with corporate platforms because even with technical feasibility, it is difficult for volunteer designers to match the quality of Big Tech's final products. This is not an insurmountable barrier, and one could foresee better-developed alternatives emerging in the future.

More difficult is the problem of user adoption in the face of the network effects of the large platforms. With corporate social media maintaining restrictions over moving friend lists and communicating across platforms, open-source projects have found it difficult to achieve the numbers needed to maintain a thriving social network. Without all of your friends and family on a platform and without the ability to communicate across platforms, it is difficult for new challengers to enter the field. One possible intervention to alleviate these problems is state-enforced mandates of data portability on the platform giants, allowing users to transfer over to different platforms and retain friend lists and personal data.

There are technical challenges here around the wide range of data that different platforms collect and the difficulties of translating this into a transferable form. There is also a privacy and legal issue about who owns different types of data. Conversations between multiple individuals on one platform, for example, could create concerns about where one person's personal information could be migrated to if another participant moved to a different platform. These issues notwithstanding, moves by dominant platforms to prevent multi-homing and switching should be placed under suspicion. Data-portability rights could enable users to change digital platforms the way you change mobile phone providers, ensuring a greater opening for democratic alternatives to emerge in this space.

Digital rights campaigner Cory Doctorow has issued a call to arms for what he calls 'adversarial interoperability': 'that's when you create a new product or service that plugs into the existing ones without the permission of the companies that make them', he claims. 'Think of third-party printer ink, alternative app stores, or independent repair shops that use compatible parts from rival manufacturers to fix your car or your phone or your tractor.'[21] Doctorow notes that many of the most important advances in communications technology occurred because of the ability of third parties to piggyback on and subvert older carriers utilising rules that forced them to interconnect with their competitors.

Mandating requirements for interoperability lowers the switching costs for users who can try out multiple platforms at the same time and communicate across them. This would create more natural flows of people between platforms and wouldn't require them to all jump at once to try a new product. If digital platforms were forced to maintain suitable application programming interfaces (APIs), which allow two applications to communicate with each other, this could provide opportunities for other platforms to plug into the dominant ones creating gateways for exodus. There would be significant challenges here because dominant players would be incentivised to undermine and subvert attempts to open them up to competitors, but there is a potential to open up greater diversity within the social media landscape.

Scaling models of decentralised systems to more than a small community of users also poses problems when having to coordinate across federated services. Past experience has shown that federal systems have slowed feature development and made it more difficult to move quickly to adapt to users' changing needs. For example, the privacy-oriented messaging app Signal decided not to adopt federated protocols because it would have been too difficult to respond to user demand and develop new features. It is hoped that with more investment in the software new methods could be developed to maintain shared protocols but enable individual nodes in the network to meet users' needs. This would be a critical aspect of enabling greater user autonomy while still maintaining the benefits of large networks.

A federal network would also allow the vague and secretive 'community standards' currently employed by corporate platforms to be democratically decided by actual communities of users. If we had many federated platforms, different communities could make their own decisions about the kinds of speech they would tolerate on their platforms. This would move decision-making power away from a gatekeeper body back towards communities.

But shifting decision-making places the burden of content moderation onto communities who may not have the resources or the desire to engage in what can often be a confronting and draining activity. This would create the need for cooperation across platforms in designing tools for moderation and identifying harmful material. Platforms have been able to cooperate in the past on certain moderation issues such as the removal of child sexual abuse material. Using a digital fingerprinting technology called photoDNA, known photos are added to a database allowing platforms to automatically prevent copies from being uploaded to their services. For hate speech and other forms of abuse, one can imagine civil liberties groups and other digital rights organisations developing software to provide filter interfaces which would allow users to determine what kind of content they see. From this perspective, we could allow dozens of content moderation systems to be trialled and learn from what approaches work best.

There are many dangers presented by a more decentralised and pluralist approach such as the growth of thought bubbles, the free rein of hate groups moderating their own networks and the increased circulation of harmful content. Although a simple and comforting option, asking Big Tech to tackle these problems in their corporate boardrooms is not the answer. We have to learn to stop trying to see these issues as technical problems that could be solved by just getting the right smart tech people in a room to design a new feature. It's not about fixing Facebook but about imagining and building an alternative – one that serves our interests, responds to our needs and over which we exercise control.

8
Recoding Our Digital Future

In the preceding chapters, I have shown how tech companies have extended the reach of their exploitative systems deeper into the social fabric of everyday life, and I have proposed an alternative based on the idea of platform socialism. Digital platforms have transformed social practices and reconfigured entire domains of human life in one of the most profound transformations since the Industrial Revolution. Tech companies have developed an unprecedented capacity to surveil and capture data from increasingly greater aspects of our social activities. This has resulted in an intensification of capitalism's underlying logic of commodifying human life. I have documented how companies use the language of community to mask their exploitative practices, exposing the prolific yet cynical PR campaigns that seek to paper over the extractive nature of platform businesses. We are likely to see more of these tactics as ideas of stakeholder capitalism and pursuing a social mission gain greater currency in the corporate world.

The approach to transformation introduced at the beginning of this book was a threefold strategy of *resisting*, *regulating* and *recoding* digital platforms. To begin with, this entails bottom-up struggles by workers and users as a method of building our power and eroding the power of tech companies. It also seeks to make use of the existing powers of the state and transnational institutions to fight the monopoly power of Big Tech and curb the worst excesses of their practices. Most importantly, however, we have emphasised a transition strategy involving the construction of alternative systems that could come to replace corporate platforms with a variety of democratic alternatives.

Challenging the system calls for a radical reformism that starts from a realistic assessment of where we are but is not restricted to solutions that appear immediately within reach. This enables us to make concrete demands that would improve the lives of those affected by digital platforms while still pushing at the boundaries of what is possible. Currently, we are a long way from where we need to be. Tech companies have solidified their position as some of the most dominant organisations on the planet and continue to pull in record profits. In spite of the recent techlash, they benefit from a lingering belief in the positive power of tech and a divided resistance movement that can't agree on what is wrong and what needs to be done. However, despite the generally bleak outlook, there are a number of promising signs that reveal deep tensions within the sector and latent conflicts that threaten to erupt.

Big Tech is widely seen as a significant threat to our privacy, freedom and democracy. This has led to populist calls for action within mainstream political discourse. This was inconceivable in the early 2010s when tech was synonymous with 'saving the world' and civilisational progress. There have also been positive developments in the tech workers' movement, with a record number of collective actions in the tech industry – 114 and 119 actions reported in 2019 and 2020 in comparison to roughly a dozen each year during the preceding decade.[1] Silicon Valley has long resisted the organisation of its workforce through a combination of surveilling workers, offering them special perks, encouraging them to see themselves as independent creative entrepreneurs and, in the final instance, firing organisers and bringing in special anti-union consultants.[2] In addition to worker organising, a number of high-profile legal cases have been brought against the largest platform companies in the US and EU which threaten to destabilise their growing dominance. What is needed at this particular juncture is for a clarification of precisely what is wrong with the way Big Tech operates and the development of an organised movement to oppose it.

EPISTEMIC RESISTANCE

Our first line of defence is epistemic resistance: we need to gain a clearer understanding of the nature of the problem and reframe the terms of the debate. Silicon Valley has been very successful at portraying itself as an irreproachable force for good. Disruption was celebrated in the name of consumer empowerment and turbocharging an on-demand economy. Even after the sector lost its glossy veneer, we have yet to escape the profound cultural influence of 'tech solutionism' – the idea that every social problem has a technological fix.[3] The starting point is recognising that the answer is not just more or better tech but a profound rethink of the political and economic systems that underpin the extractive platform economy. We should consult existing bodies of literature on technology and society rather than celebrating historically illiterate tech insiders turned critics.

There are currently multiple frames through which groups conceptualise the problems of Big Tech based on different strategic interests and political priorities. Incensed by the Cambridge Analytica scandal and other data breaches, many liberals are concerned with surveillance and the violation of individuals' rights to privacy. Conservatives are also concerned about privacy but worry about censorship and controls on free speech due to the perceived left-wing political bias of Silicon Valley. Across the political spectrum, citizens are concerned about the levels of misinformation spread on social media and the corrosive effect this has on public debate. More generally, tech sceptics believe that social media platforms are subtly manipulating and controlling us through behaviour modification techniques. In the economic sphere, there are also concerns about anticompetitive practices by Big Tech firms competing in markets they control and using their monopoly power to crush competition. When people complain about the problems of Big Tech, it's likely they have a range of these issues in mind.

Drawing on these frames, we can see that there are important points of overlap and shared concerns which can act as catalysts for shifting the discourse. Most people consider large tech companies to be too big, too powerful and a danger to democracy. There is bipartisan support in the US for action to be taken to reduce the concentration of their power. When we talk about issues of Big Tech's dominance, we need to push for more robust forms of democratic control to be incorporated into digital platforms. Many of the seemingly isolated issues such as misinformation, social media addiction and online harassment stem from the profit-driven structure of the companies. We should be talking more about the root causes of the problems and how the platforms themselves could be redesigned to suit the public's needs rather than just how the worst evils of their practices could be minimised.

Education and media literacy campaigns will be one small but important part of the solution. It's not just a question of educating engineers on social and political issues but about educating all citizens to play a more active role in influencing the design and implementation of new technology. We need to engage communities that are directly impacted by the use of technology and learn more from the history of previous technological innovations. Lilly Irani and Rumman Chowdhury write:

Real problem solving means engaging those impacted communities at the design phase and beyond, even if it means putting an end to some projects. Rather than leading with tech principles, developers must work with experienced groups to develop true 'human-centric' design – in which the human is more than just the average Silicon Valley resident.[4]

Education campaigns can be organised as collective acts of solidarity, such as the 'Our Data Bodies' project – a research and education initiative which produced a set of community power tools for reclaiming citizens' data sovereignty.[5] The idea behind this project and other similar initiatives is to understand how communities, particularly those marginalised by race, gender, class, sexuality and immigration status, are impacted by data-based technologies. It is an attempt to build social movements for data justice and to involve communities in reflecting on how these technologies affect their lives.

WORKERS' RESISTANCE

Building our discursive power can only get us so far. Resisting the power of Big Tech must also come from workers within tech companies. It is easy to be pessimistic about the possibility of collective forms of workers' resistance in the platform economy today. Platforms seem uniquely designed to atomise workers, force them into competition with one another and prevent them from building associational power. Tech work is hierarchically divided between well-paid, full-time employees, service workers employed by subcontracted companies and 'independent contractors' performing platform labour tasks who are often algorithmically managed and have little direct contact with either human managers or other workers.[6] These workers also labour under unprecedented regimes of surveillance and data extraction. Their routines are closely monitored and the platforms often disrupt or suppress workers' communication with each other and reduce their capacity to share information and organise collectively. For platform labourers, the low entry barrier to working for labour platforms and the continuous influx of new workers undermines their bargaining power and makes it difficult to plausibly threaten to withdraw their labour.

However, in spite of the difficulties, a new wave of workers' mobilisation in the platform economy has emerged with promising avenues for the cooperation of new tech worker collectives, informal worker organisations, grassroots unions and traditional larger unions.[7] Recruitment and organising is perhaps most difficult among isolated platform workers. Nevertheless, food delivery riders organised pickets and strikes across European cities from 2016 to 2017, which has been an effective method of pressuring platform companies. Callum Cant has shown that organising a highly fragmented and isolated workforce poses extra challenges, but riders have been finding ways to create new communities of resistance using WhatsApp groups and gathering in informal waiting zones outside clusters of restaurants.[8] Survey data from ride hail drivers has demonstrated that participation in online communities with other drivers increased their desire to join a workers' collective and improved their views of unions more generally.[9]

The situation varies across different national contexts, but traditional larger unions have been reluctant to engage with workers deemed 'unorganisable' in the platform economy leaving independent grassroots unions to step up their organising.[10] Unions such as the Independent Workers Union of Great Britain (IWGB), the Free Workers' Union in Germany and Örestad LS in Sweden have supported groups of riders in their respective countries.[11] Elsewhere, platform workers have sought to organise through their own organisations, such as the California App-Based Drivers Association, which is a not-for-profit membership association promoting fairness, justice and transparency for drivers in the ride hail industry. Similarly, in early 2020, London witnessed the first meeting of the International Alliance of App-Based Transport Workers with participants from 23 different countries.[12]

Deliveroo in the UK has refused to negotiate in formal collective bargaining with union representatives from the IWGB. However, other countries have had more success. In January 2021, the Danish Chamber of Commerce and 3F Transport made a collective agreement for food delivery couriers resulting in regulated wages, sick pay, holiday pay and pensions.[13] This agreement was signed by Just Eat and applies to its 600 couriers that gained coverage under this agreement. Collective agreements guaranteeing workers minimum wages, guaranteed hours and benefits are possible and should be struggled for across the globe. It is a fiction that workers cannot have flexibility in their work schedule alongside proper labour rights and protections.

Workers operating in private homes offering (female-dominated) domestic cleaning and care services face additional hurdles to engaging in collective resistance. First, their private workplaces offer less opportunities to meet and organise with other workers.[14] There is also evidence that care work platforms are more likely than delivery and ride hail platforms to seek to formalise employment relationships through technologies that increase the visibility of workers to clients.[15] Workers on care platforms such as Care.com are not automatically assigned to new clients but are selected based on reviews, making collective action more difficult and risky. Similarly, extra hurdles exist for immigrants and undocumented workers – many of whom already work in highly precarious conditions and are forced onto platforms due to the comparatively lower entry barriers into this segment of the labour market.[16]

Some traditional unions have also reached out to platform workers. IG Metall, Germany's largest union, launched the 'Fair Crowd Work' initiative in 2016, which provides assistance to crowd workers on platforms such as Amazon Mechanical Turk not formally affiliated with a union.[17] More recently, IG Metall has partnered with a group of professional content creators on YouTube to establish 'FairTube'. Beginning as an informal agreement to cooperate in July 2019, the joint venture solidified into an official union at the end of 2020.[18] It now campaigns for greater fairness and transparency with regards to YouTube's recommendation algorithm and payment processes. YouTube has been reluctant to acknowledge the existence of anything resembling a union among its creator community. As in other parts of the platform economy, this partnership could point towards new developments in worker organising and ways for those without employment contracts to engage in collective action.

Full-time white-collar workers and subcontracted workers within the sector have also become more vocal in recent years. This has included organising from warehouse workers, cafeteria staff and security guards in addition to programmers and software developers. Amazon warehouse workers in Alabama have pushed for the creation of a union, which would be the first time an entire Amazon warehouse was unionised and is also the biggest union drive in the south of the United States in years.[19]

White-collar workers have tended to be more muted in their organising, employing naming and shaming tactics and focusing on particularly egregious examples of poor behaviour or unethical projects within their companies. However, even at Google, which has vigorously pursued anti-union efforts, workers formed the Alphabet Workers' Union in

January 2021, a non-contract or 'solidarity' union.[20] What is most promising about this emerging movement is the attempt to build bonds of solidarity across different sectors and different types of work. Developing these cross-cutting forms of solidarity will be crucial to growing the strength of the movement. Existing social media apps such as Signal provide the possibility for workers to organise and build power in ways that cannot be tracked and monitored by the large platform companies. Groups such as the Tech Workers' Coalition have been instrumental in forming alliances between white-collar employees and independent contractors working in the tech sector, helping to train and organise workers through workshops and forums.[21] Given the heterogeneity of these organisational forms and different methods of building workers' collective power, it's still too early to tell which experiments will prove most effective. It's unlikely that there is any single model that will be the future of worker resistance since each form has been adapted to suit its own context.

It will be important for all tech workers to be supported by wider social movements willing to put pressure on companies and support workers' demands. Activists within political parties should also aim to pressure party leaders to place pro-worker policies related to technology in their manifestos. The British Labour Party proposed an ambitious collection of tech policies in its 2019 manifesto which promised full fibre broadband for all citizens, increased investment in research and development (3 per cent of gross domestic product by 2030) and a Green Industrial Revolution. This was due to important work by party activists ensuring that reforms made it onto the party's agenda by maintaining pressure from below. Collective action by tech workers used to be rare, but there are signs that the antagonism between platform owners and workers will continue to mount in the 2020s, which could lead to the development of more radical claims by workers.

REGULATING BIG TECH

The movement towards a democratic platform economy also requires action from regulatory institutions to curb the worst excesses of tech companies and to rein in their power. Many of the current demands of precarious workers involve the state guaranteeing proper employment contracts and working conditions. Local and municipal institutions may serve as ideal locations for new participatory structures of certain forms of platform governance, but concerted effort is needed at the level of the state to adequately regulate current multinational companies. States have a key role to play here because they have the power to create new regulatory frameworks, fine companies that break the rules and break up big tech monopolies.

It can seem like platforms have become new global entities that transcend national boundaries and exist in a parallel universe. But as Mark Graham has argued, platforms are necessarily embedded in one geographic context or another – their offices, workers and tax bills all end up sitting within particular jurisdictions.[22] Companies try to exploit existing loopholes and allowances to pay as little tax as possible and avoid regulations by claiming they are merely digital intermediaries, but states could tighten up the current exceptions utilised by these companies.

One level of regulations that are urgently required are stronger employment law protections for precarious workers who often fall outside of existing frameworks. Platform labour researcher Niels van Doorn has argued for a need to end the pervasive 'platform exceptionalism' in which platform companies are treated as unique businesses able to avoid regulations yet still control a labour force through systems of algorithmic management.[23] Globally, platform companies thrive in countries with institutionally weak environments in which they can exploit loopholes and weaknesses in legal frameworks. National legislation is needed to close down the possibility of precarious workers being classified as independent contractors who bear all the risks of their work for the platform. Gig workers would benefit from guaranteed worker protections with a right to minimum guaranteed hours, a minimum wage, sick and holiday pay and collective bargaining. Platform companies should not be allowed to bypass two centuries of struggle and take workers back to nineteenth-century levels of precarity.

We should expect platform companies to oppose any attempts to properly classify workers as employees. In California, platform companies poured over US$200 million into their lobbying efforts to pass Proposition 22, which gave the companies an exemption to Assembly Bill 5, allowing them to classify their drivers as independent contractors. This was a grave defeat for precarious workers, but it won't be the last time the issue is put to legislators or the people. Uber is already attempting to reproduce their strategy for driver reclassification at the European level, hoping to gain an exemption for their workers that would enable the company not to provide the benefits and protections of employment. Countering this threat, Phil Jones has written persuasively on the importance of a new regime of universal workers' rights regardless of a workers' status:

> In an age where arrangements like the gig economy and microwork are testing the very legal definitions upon which the labour market rests; where employees are in decline and the self-employed on the rise; and where a highly interconnected world means all workers face the same global risks – pandemics and climate catastrophe – we need a system of universal rights that no longer privileges certain segments of the labour market, but provides the same safety net and benefits for all.[24]

We need new legislation that makes it clear that companies cannot find loopholes to exploit vulnerable classes of workers and erode the existing protections available to full-time employees.

Platform workers want to escape precarity while still retaining the flexibility to work around their schedules. Reclassification alone would not solve the broader questions of vulnerable workers across low-wage industries. What is needed is better protections for workers – from higher minimum wages to more security in their work – who find themselves in the bottom end of the labour market and who are subject to predatory behaviour from unscrupulous businesses.

We should also rethink the general approach that allows companies to have a seemingly unlimited right to surveil their workers in the workplace. National legislators could enforce strict limits on the extent to which workers are allowed to be monitored and surveilled. Autonomous craftsmen in late nineteenth-century America safeguarded their collective control over the labour process by refusing to work when their bosses were watching.[25] They rightly saw that this surveillance was part of a larger system of scientific management designed to discipline workers and squeeze higher levels of productivity from them. Today, the technology to monitor and time every task has enabled Amazon to enforce an inhuman pace of work in their warehouses, leading 66 per cent of employees asked in one survey to report experiencing physical pain while performing their work duties.[26] Regulation to prevent such extremes would help level the playing field and facilitate workers exercising more control over the rhythm of their work.

Additional regulatory action can be taken on other issues to reduce the concentration of the power of Big Tech companies, beginning with mergers. An antitrust agenda is currently being revived in the US, drawing on lessons from New Deal-era reformers who used the Sherman and Clayton Antitrust Acts to limit the power of large companies.[27] Despite the limitations of the antitrust cases identified in previous chapters, the US federal government should pursue the unwinding of tech empires such as the mergers between Facebook, WhatsApp and Instagram as a first step towards reducing their monopoly power.

Predatory and unfair business practices by large tech companies should also be investigated. As a preliminary measure, companies such as Amazon and Google should not be able to use data from their own marketplaces to dominate their competitors using their service. Reforms suggested by European authorities, such as the Digital Markets Act, seek to prevent these gatekeeper businesses from using their special powers to engage in anticompetitive behaviour. These reforms are a step in the right direction, but the business models of large platform companies do not only harm competition. Additional behavioural rules will be needed that protect citizens' personal data and institute greater transparency in how the platforms currently operate.

We might also like to consider regulations stipulating absolute size limitations either in relative terms of market share or in absolute terms related to the company's overall valuation or annual profit. In the short term, we could incentivise companies not to grow above a certain size of the market by implementing significantly higher tax brackets for companies that breach this threshold.

As a step towards democratic ownership and control, companies that provide a service to the public should be designated as public utilities and regulated as such. In the US, public service commissions should be established with the specific scope of regulating this new class of digital platforms to ensure they provide a decent service in exchange for a fair price. The commission should investigate the 'data for a free service' model of many of these companies and determine how appropriate protections can be developed for users. In particular, social media platforms have evaded responsibility for what users post on their platform. Moves to rewrite Section 230 of the Communications Decency Act are therefore welcome, although, at the time of writing, it is still unclear what direction this will take and whether the proposed redrafting could have potentially unintended consequences.

Another important regulation would be for platform companies to be compelled to share their data with public authorities. Having access to this data is a crucial step in determining the real effects of platforms on urban life and in better understanding what needs to change. This is particularly the case in the short-term rental market where governments can intervene to tackle negative effects on housing prices and community life. As part of the EU's legislative proposal of the Digital Services Act, submitted to the European Parliament on 15 December 2020, the Dutch deputy prime minister called for new rules to enforce greater data sharing with government.[28]

One major limitation of a regulatory approach to challenging the power of Big Tech has been the success of these companies in lobbying regulators and influencing how regulations are framed. Furthermore, even in cases where seemingly effective regulations are in place, they do not always influence companies' behaviour. The EU Commission's antitrust actions against Alphabet – which have even resulted in fines in excess of a billion dollars – have not worked as a deterrent on their behaviour or had any effect on the company's market value.[29]

Big Tech companies have also spent large sums paying lobbyists to influence EU decisions and create regulations in their favour. A report from Corporate Europe Observatory found that short-term rental platform companies fought against European cities' measures to protect affordable housing by lobbying the EU Commission.[30] The report found that lobbyists had frequent contact with regulators, that significant concessions had already been made and that Airbnb had filed official complaints against several European cities to the Commission. It's in Big Tech's interest to spend big on lobbyists because the regulations have a serious impact on the viability of their business model. This means that regulation will always have to be pursued through harnessing the power of a bottom-up people's movement to put pressure on regulators to make decisions in the best interests of the public.

Ultimately, regulations are a necessary but not sufficient condition for the transformation of the platform economy. Regulations that protect workers, enhance their bargaining position and strengthen their rights to privacy should be championed. However, we lose a vital ingredient in an ambitious reform agenda when the problem is understood purely in terms of the need for new legislation and lawsuits. Increased competition in the sector should not be our ultimate goal. Dozens of mini-Facebooks still operating on a similar model will not fundamentally transform the underlying problems of the digital economy. We should take advantage of the current momentum behind antitrust actions by forming tactical alliances with those who also want to reduce the power of Big Tech companies. But the liberal agenda of strengthening markets and enhancing competition runs counter to our ultimate goal of creating and sustaining non-market forms of coordinating economic activities.

RECODING BIG TECH

So long as we are wedded to the idea that the future will be controlled by a handful of enormous companies, we won't be able to envision genuine alternatives. Throughout this book we have stressed the importance of constructing institutional designs that would empower voluntary associations in civil society to exercise effective control over digital platforms. In order to recode Big Tech, we can't be satisfied with just fixing the platforms we have. We need to imagine how we can build and support alternatives that will be able to grow and sustain themselves in the long term as centres of social power.

This book has focused on the importance of digital infrastructure as the foundation of the platform economy and that which enables tech companies to exercise their dominance over the system. Without control over this infrastructural layer, transitioning to alternative platforms may not be possible. We need infrastructure embedded with a new set of values to code an egalitarian logic into the design of new systems.

Drawing on the framework of sociologist Eric Olin Wright, this strategy could be characterised as one of *interstitial transformation*: building radical democratic institutions within the 'cracks' of the capitalist system with a view to eroding the dominance of capitalist institutions.[31] This view of transformation emphasises the importance of developing an alternative base of power and the need to gain a foothold within capitalism for different kinds of social relations to grow. Over a period of protracted struggle and the development of new centres of power, the egalitarian institutions could come to challenge capitalist ones for their hegemonic position in society. In this view, one of the preconditions of transformation is the growth of a network of democratically run organisations in which active citizens exercise direct control over production and exchange. The creation of robust forms of economic democracy would lead to a situation in which there were competing logics for how economic power was exercised in society. Elements of capitalism might remain in new hybrid configurations as the logic of profit making became subordinated to the growing movement for democratic control over economic activity.

Wright's reflections on theories of transformation are particularly pertinent to platform socialism because many of the examples of emerging 'real utopias' he championed were taken from internet-based forms of organisation. He characterises Wikipedia as an example of a non-capitalist form of knowledge production that exists alongside other forms on the internet. He also drew inspiration from online strategies to subvert capitalist intellectual property rights such as music sharing sites and free and open-source software.

The primary contradiction of this strategy of interstitial transformation is that the growth of alternatives would be strongly opposed by elites whose interests were threatened by transformation. Small-scale alternatives would be tolerated and even encouraged as convenient pressure release valves for the system. But as soon as alternatives began to threaten real change, elites would exercise their power to block and subvert them.

The problem of elite resistance is one that any theory of transformation is forced to confront. The best response is to strengthen democratic alternatives within the system and to extend and deepen democratic forms of organisation within capitalist societies to compete for hegemony over social institutions. The first step to challenging these powerful interests is to imagine possible futures that they do not control. Only then will we be able to build a thriving ecosystem of democratic alternatives to reclaim our digital future.

Postscript: 2042

Yasmine hated mornings. Even with an app that monitored her sleep and woke her at an optimal time, she still deeply resented getting out of bed to start the day. It was her first day at a new job at the mayor of London's office and she was excited to face the challenges that lay ahead. She'd been hired to redesign the city's notoriously dilapidated public transport system. She felt this was a turning point and that these first days with her new team would shape the contours of the new world they hoped to create.

As Yasmine showered, the AI in her bathroom conducted its daily automated tests for a range of diseases. This data automatically uploaded to her MyHealth account on the Platform, which was supplemented by data from her wearable health monitors throughout the day. She thought about how relieved she was not to be in the US, where information on her psoriasis and dairy intolerance would cause a hike in her insurance payments. As she dried off, Yasmine reviewed her activity and diet tracker from the previous day, checking her key wellness indicators. She was now 43 and could see she was doing OK healthwise compared to others in her age bracket.

There wasn't much in Yasmine's life that wasn't tracked by one system or another. Details of her life were constantly uploaded to the Cloud. Data came primarily from the ubiquitous sensors on her devices and in her house. But it was also sourced from public spaces now equipped with facial recognition technology that could recognise movements, branded clothes, even facial expressions – all of which was churned into data, insight and profit.

Yasmine had taught herself how to do hair and makeup as a young adult. She still enjoyed the ritual each morning and assembled all of her instruments in a row on her desk. As she applied each product, she scrolled through the Feed on her smart mirror. The Feed was a digest of everything she needed for the day, from tech and transport news, to personal messages from friends and family – all combined with the latest articles, music and movies recommended by the algorithm. The Platform's system of 'artisanal automation' boasted sophisticated algorithms that worked alongside human 'taste makers' who would hand pick a selection of content that cut through the noise of the web.

As a premium subscriber, Yasmine could click on new products advertised on the Feed and they would arrive in her personal delivery box later that day. Of course, it didn't always get things right. It once incessantly pushed different hiking boots immediately after Yasmine purchased a pair, which seemed like the last moment at which she would have a need for new ones.

The Feed had also become her main line of connection to her friends and family. She could communicate for free through the social infrastructure of the Platform. It was increasingly difficult to tell the difference between social media, finance, work and entertainment. It had all been integrated into the same convenient network. Day-to-day activities such as paying bills, booking appointments and chatting with friends all took place alongside branded videos and push notifications of new items that would improve her life. It wasn't like people had been forced to use the Platform's many apps. They were just so convenient and well designed.

In fact, the Platform took care of most of her needs, with around 70 per cent of her salary debited directly to the company each month. This included groceries, mortgage payments, mobile and internet bills, entertainment subscriptions and most of her shopping. Yasmine's two miniature dachshunds, Barcus Aurelius and Karl Barx, also took full advantage of the service. They too disliked mornings and watched her get ready from a comfy position on the couch. They were rather spoiled, as far as dogs go, receiving many treats and two walks a day while she was at work through the Platform's dog minding app, Doggo.

One of her closest friends from her Stanford days had been one of the Feeds' lead designers. Like others of their generation who grew up during the exuberance and excess of the Streaming Twenties, Yasmine and her friends were filled with a sense of urgency about the need for radical change. Once the world was vaccinated from Covid-19, it was as if a decade of culture and creativity was released all at once. A cultural renaissance occurred alongside the ongoing climate catastrophe and creeping nationalism and militarisation due to new resource wars.

Gen P, as they were called – although nobody could decide whether the P stood for pandemic or platform – had grown distrustful of a world they felt was built to control them rather than let them be free. The tech gurus of the 2010s, it had turned out, were not so different from their baby boomer parents – they too had grown old and defensive of the world they had created and resented the brashness and impertinence of the next generation.

Although she did not come from privilege, Yasmine's natural adaptability, and a full tuition scholarship, gave her a foothold into a competitive world of dreams and aspiration. She had been attracted to the precision and rigour of STEM subjects and appreciated the real-world challenges they seemed to address. California felt like the centre of this mythic world and finding a way to get there became her obsession.

Yasmine was a former refugee from Iraq and this often left her feeling out of place in Stanford. This only fuelled her drive to compete and prove herself in this new environment. No point standing on the side of the road with a placard. If things were going to change, it would be through people like her working on the inside. As a student, she didn't have a clear idea of what that change would be. Making it into this world felt like a political act. She didn't think she was smart enough or that she would fit in with the culture, but she wanted to be part of a group of people who would go on to change the world.

These weird insecurities and competitiveness all seemed so silly now. Her lucrative career in tech meant that she was one of the lucky few who could still afford to buy a house. As well-off millennials inherited their parents' wealth, the divide between the rich and poor had grown. Few were able to afford to buy without good careers or help from their parents. Social housing had been further squeezed, with over half of the government's stock sold off to private developers during the 2020s, placing further pressure on housing lists. In response, social entrepreneurs funded by the Platform's charity arm had invented low-cost self-inflating makeshift shelters which were now littered across the city as a visible sign of the rising housing problem.

Yasmine decided to schedule some dinner for later that night as she knew she would not be home in time to cook anything decent. The main food delivery businesses had first merged and then been bought up and integrated into a larger food production supply chain. The Platform now made its own food in cloud kitchens with no storefronts or seating. It provided the most popular options of burgers, pizzas, poké and grilled harissa chicken on its app. Years of consumer data enabled the Platform to refine its recommended menu to these most popular dishes. Despite also offering a wide range of other options, the algorithm pushed the recommended selection and people chose these over 90 per cent of the time. The orders were fully customisable and easy to produce. The food production process had been automated and delivery was made by a fleet of drones. The Platform had reduced the cost of meal preparation and delivery to £1, which allowed the company to lower the price of food and take in a greater margin due to supply chain savings. Orders arrived with free sample products and advertisements for the Platform's many other services.

The Platform was the English name of a Chinese conglomerate that had been formed in the late 2020s through the merger of three of China's biggest e-commerce and cloud platforms. The American platforms were still at war with government regulators and it was several years before they were able to merge to form Prime. Social media apps had become a new landscape for political propaganda and cultural competition. The adoption of the Platform's social media app, Me2, by billions of Western users was a huge coup for the Chinese government. Fuelled by the rising currency of Chinese fashion and culture, the Platform had shot up in popularity with younger users. Beijing and Bangalore now saw more start-up investment money than Silicon Valley or other US tech hubs. Despite still having billions of users, Prime's platform had stagnated and was mainly used by older generations who still referred to its competitor as the 'Chinese Platform' with an air of derision.

Most of Yasmine's friends had a Platform subscription, although some were also with Prime for the extra discounts and benefits. Yasmine couldn't stand Prime. Not because there was anything wrong with the service per se, but mainly for how she was treated there early in her career. She had accepted an offer for a position at the company right after grad school. Prime's slogan was 'changing the world, for good'. Their eager new recruits were exceptionally well paid and were made to feel like they had earned it. During lunch breaks they relaxed in comfortable cafeterias and on Fridays they received pep talks from their company's now-ageing founders.

But within a few months at the company, work had become an unsatisfying grind. While she had been invited to appear at a number of public-facing events as the minority lead in this or that area, her research was often overlooked or ignored. More seemed to be expected of her and there was less room for error. During her first years, she published a number of high-profile studies on the intersections of tech and social policy and blitzed her performance reviews. But she still felt constantly scrutinised and her managers treated her differently than other colleagues with pure tech backgrounds. Sometimes she was just left out of conversations altogether. While in theory the company was dedicated to increasing the number of people like Yasmine, in practice, diversity statistics had never significantly improved in the entire history of the company.

She started an internal group for women of colour at Prime who talked about the lack of diversity and unequal treatment of black and brown workers at tech companies. Conversations in the group also addressed employees' lack of autonomy in the firm, and the way the industry negatively affected local communities. The city had become more segregated and people seemed to exist in parallel worlds. Some zipped around on electric scooters, living in expensive condos and drinking branded water, while others commuted two hours to work and worked 80-hour weeks on zero-hour contracts. Yasmine also saw how many women of colour outside of tech were forced to work in insecure jobs which left them feeling physically and emotionally exhausted.

Most low-paid workers were now on WorkIt, an app which stored all their employment history and anonymous ratings from previous employers. While the software made job applications faster, most workers were too scared to confront their bosses due to fears of low ratings on their record. People of colour were twice as likely to have negative feedback from former employers.

Despite the many problems Yasmine faced at the company, she pioneered Prime's autonomous vehicle programme and developed this technology for the company's transportation and on-demand delivery services. Over the next eight years, she became a transport tech expert and supported a new generation of women of colour in the firm. But her experience at Prime radicalised her. Seeing how things worked from the inside showed her that the company – and the system it was a part of – was beyond reform. There were some great people in the company who genuinely believed they were making the world a better place by solving humanity's problems through technology. But the pressure to compete against other firms drove the company in a bad direction. Often, new employees wanted to see themselves as changing things for the better, but the company's leadership was all about revenue, engagement and growth.

The growing inequality of the platform economy and the precarity that it bred led to mounting pressure for something to be done. The big platform companies tried to hide the dark underbelly of their businesses, but this was getting increasingly difficult with more workers organising and resisting. Microworkers labelling data for pennies in sheds in special tech zones in the world's poorest cities created a new global union and began organising alongside traditional labour unions. Social movements against the companies' exploitative model had been galvanised by several high-profile legal cases against the big platforms, which had forced them to disclose damning internal memos about the company's plans to build global empires and suppress their competition. The power of the tech companies had increased dramatically, but so too had movements opposing their dominance.

Last year, the catalyst finally arrived. Prime accidentally deleted the records of 127 low-income users from their servers in a routine clean up. Suddenly, those individuals' access to essential services had been shut off. The records had been so thoroughly erased that there was no evidence they had ever existed in the system. Their weekly payments for housing ended alongside their food payments, access to health facilities and communications services. Credit ratings plummeted almost instantly, resulting in applications for credit and housing being rejected. For the most vulnerable, this meant homelessness and destitution. For the chronically ill and disabled, it meant the erasure of years of treatments, therapies and information required to access welfare and support services.

By the time the error was corrected two months later, a dozen of these people had lost their lives. A woman's body was found in one of the branded makeshift shelters provided by the company whose failure had taken their life. Prime's senior management freaked out and tried to cover up the incident, but a tape from their meeting was leaked. A voice could be heard saying something about a wartime CEO seeing these deaths as necessary casualties of war and that it would ultimately be a small bump in the road as the company reached seven billion users. A wave of outrage rippled across the globe. Protestors burned the offices of big platform companies, while unions and social movements led rallies across major cities. For years, people had demanded change from these companies, but this moment felt different. Human life had literally been deleted from the planet. The discourse had shifted and people marched on the streets with signs reading 'Platform Democracy Now!' Yasmine joined the protests and spread the message among her friends, hoping to get as many people out as possible.

Spurred on by the mass movements, global leaders voiced their disgust at the actions of the company and vowed to take action. People demanded more control over how the platforms functioned and wanted to put an end to the exploitative practices of the companies. Plans were rapidly put into action to bring the platforms back under control and for people across the world to reclaim their digital sovereignty.

Yasmine had quit Prime the year before the protests in a widely publicised dispute with Prime's CEO. She had criticised a new contract the company had signed with the Department of Defense to begin a weapons programme involving the company's autonomous vehicles. Since then, she had designed a number of tools of digital labour activism and worked with organisations advocating for justice in the platform economy. The mayor's chief of staff had invited her along with other organisers and tech experts to an emergency meeting about how the city could respond to the crisis. A global trend towards devolution had empowered municipal authorities with larger budgets and remits for their work.

As she stood on the train on her way to work, Yasmine surveyed the underinvestment in public infrastructure and the vast inequalities that now pervaded her city. She considered how the city could find new ways of organising the platform economy. The moment felt historic in some way. She thought about how others before her might have imagined her world in 2042 and if this is what they had wanted. She also wondered if others had tried do things differently but had been thwarted – as she might be – by doubts about what was truly possible.

Notes

INTRODUCTION

1. See Shoshana Zuboff, *The Age of Surveillance Capitalism: The Fight for a Human Future at the New Frontier of Power* (New York: Profile Books, 2019).
2. David Leopold, 'On Marxian Utopophobia', *Journal of the History of Philosophy* 54, no. 1 (2016), pp. 111–34.
3. Mark Fisher, *Capitalist Realism: Is There No Alternative?* (London: Zero Books, 2009).
4. Miguel Abensour, 'William Morris: The Politics of Romance', in Max Blechman (ed.), *Revolutionary Romanticism* (San Francisco: City Lights Books, 1999), p. 145.
5. Isaiah Berlin, 'Two Concepts of Liberty', in *Four Essays on Liberty* (Oxford: Oxford University Press, 1969), p. 122.
6. Annelien de Dijn, *Freedom: An Unruly History* (Cambridge, MA: Harvard University Press, 2020).
7. Angela Davis, *Freedom Is a Constant Struggle: Ferguson, Palestine and the Foundations of a Movement* (Chicago: Haymarket Books, 2016). See also James Muldoon, 'Freedom as Collective Self-determination', in *Building Power to Change the World* (Oxford: Oxford University Press, 2020), 52–72.
8. Phil Jones, *Work without the Worker: Labour in the Age of Platform Capitalism* (London: Verso, 2021).
9. Michael Kwet, 'Digital Colonialism: US Empire and the New Imperialism in the Global South', *Race & Class* 60, no. 4 (2019), pp. 4–26.
10. Catherine D'Ignazio and Lauren F. Klein, *Data Feminism* (Cambridge, MA: MIT Press, 2020); Safiya Umoja Noble, *Algorithms of Oppression: How Search Engines Reinforce Racism* (New York: NYU Press, 2018).
11. Wendy Liu, *Abolish Silicon Valley* (London: Repeater Books, 2020).
12. For the outlines of a similar strategic perspective, see Mark Graham, 'Regulate, Replicate, and Resist – the Conjunctural Geographies of Platform Urbanism', *Urban Geography* 41, no. 3 (2020).

CHAPTER 1

1. Arun Sundararajan, *The Sharing Economy: The End of Employment and the Rise of Crowd-Based Capitalism* (Cambridge, MA: MIT Press, 2016).
2. Trebor Scholz, *Uberworked and Underpaid: How Workers Are Disrupting the Digital Economy* (New York: Wiley, 2016).

3. Ursula Huws et al., 'The Platformisation of Work in Europe: Results from Research in 13 European Countries' (Brussels: Foundation for European Progressive Studies, UNI Europa, and University of Hertfordshire, 2019), p. 22.

4. Casey Newton, 'Mark in the Metaverse', *The Verge*, 22 July 2021. www.theverge.com/22588022/mark-zuckerberg-facebook-ceo-metaverse-interview (all URLs accessed August 2021).

5. Matthew Ball, 'The Metaverse: What It Is, Where to Find It, Who Will Build It, and Fortnite', 21 January 2020. www.matthewball.vc/all/themetaverse.

6. This occurred to a South African Uber driver who discovered he had contracted with Uber International Holdings BV, a Netherlands-based company, leading to his case being dismissed. *Mokhutswane* v. *Uber South Africa (Pty) Ltd* [2019] ZANCT 64. www.saflii.org/za/cases/ZANCT/2019/64.html.

7. UBS, 'Billionaire's Insights 2020'. www.pwc.com.au/private-clients/assets/ubs-billionaires-insights-2020.pdf.

8. Gavriella Schuster, 'The Digital First Responder Opportunity with Microsoft', *Microsoft blog*. https://blogs.partner.microsoft.com/mpn/the-digital-first-responder-opportunity-with-microsoft/.

9. See Steven Vallas and Juliet Schor, 'What Do Platforms Do? Understanding the Gig Economy', *Annual Review of Sociology* 46 (2020), pp. 273–94. For an early and influential typology see Nick Srnicek, *Platform Capitalism* (London: Polity, 2016).

10. David Curry, 'Apple Statistics (2021)', *Business of Apps*. www.businessofapps.com/data/apple-statistics/.

11. Spenser Soper, 'Amazon Building Global Delivery Business to Take on Alibaba', *Bloomberg*, 9 February 2016. www.bloomberg.com/news/articles/2016-02-09/amazon-is-building-global-delivery-business-to-take-on-alibaba-ikfhpyes.

12. The caveat is that all three features do not apply equally to each of the different types of platforms.

13. This definition is adopted from Christophers, *Rentier Capitalism* (London: Verso, 2020), p. 41. See also Kean Birch, 'Technoscience Rent: Towards a Theory of Rentiership in Technoscientific Capitalism', *Science, Technology and Human Values* 45, no. 1 (2020), pp. 3–33.

14. Ibid., 50.

15. David Lynch, 'Rising Stock Market Would Be in the Red without a Handful of Familiar Names', *Washington Post*, 20 August 2020. www.washingtonpost.com/business/2020/08/19/tech-stocks-markets/.

16. Ibid.

17. Vallas and Schor, 'What Do Platforms Do? Understanding the Gig Economy'.

18. Alex Rosenblat and Luke Stark. 'Algorithmic Labor and Information Asymmetries: A Case Study of Uber's Drivers', *International Journal of Communication* 10 (2016), pp. 3758–84.

19. Niels van Doorn, 'Platform Labor: On the Gendered and Racialized Exploitation of Low-Income Service Work in the 'On-demand' Economy', *Information, Communications, Society* 20, no. 6 (2017), pp. 898–914.

20. Juliet B. Schor, William Attwood-Charles, Mehmet Cansoy, Isak Ladegaard and Robert Wengronowitz, 'Dependence and Precarity in the Platform Economy', *Theory and Society* 49 (2020), pp. 833–61.

21. Juliet B. Schor, *After the Gig: How the Sharing Economy Got Hijacked and How to Win It Back* (Oakland: University of California Press, 2020), p. 121.

22. Rodrigo Fernandez, Ilke Adriaans, Tobias J. Klinge and Reijer Hendrikse, 'Engineering Digital Monopolies: The Financialisation of Big Tech', Centre for Research on Multinational Corporations (December 2020), p. 9.

23. Ibid.

24. Ibid.

25. Srnicek, *Platform Capitalism*; United Nations, 'Digital Economy Report 2019 – Value Creation and Capture: Implications for Developing Countries', UNTCAD (2019); Jathan Sadowski, *Too Smart: How Digital Capitalism Is Extracting Data, Controlling Our Lives, and Taking over the World* (Cambridge, MA: MIT Press, 2020), pp. 25–37.

26. Jathan Sadowski, 'When Data Is Capital: Datafication, Accumulation, and Extraction', *Big Data & Society* (2019), pp. 1–12.

27. *The Economist*, 'The World's Most Valuable Resource Is No Longer Oil, But Data', 6 May 2017. www.economist.com/leaders/2017/05/06/the-worlds-most-valuable-resource-is-no-longer-oil-but-data; Kiran Bhageshpur, 'Data Is the New Oil – And That's a Good Thing', *Forbes*, 15 November 2019. www.forbes.com/sites/forbestechcouncil/2019/11/15/data-is-the-new-oil-and-thats-a-good-thing/.

28. Lisa Gitelman, ed., *'Raw Data' Is an Oxymoron* (Cambridge, MA: MIT Press, 2013).

29. Antonio Garcia Martinez, 'No, Data Is Not the New Oil', *Wired*, 26 February 2019. www.wired.com/story/no-data-is-not-the-new-oil/.

30. Karl Marx coined the term 'commodity fetishism' to refer to how we obscure the social relations through which goods and services are produced as if commodities themselves had a completely independent existence. See Karl Marx, *Capital*, Vol. 1 (London: Penguin Books, 1990), ch. 1.

31. Ofcom, 'UK's Internet Use Surges to Record Levels', 20 June 2020. www.ofcom.org.uk/about-ofcom/latest/media/media-releases/2020/uk-internet-use-surges.

32. Salome Viljoen, 'Democratic Data: A Relational Theory for Data Governance', 23 November 2020. https://papers.ssrn.com/sol3/papers.cfm?abstract_id=3727562.

33. Mario Tronti, 'The Factory and Society', *Quaderni Rossi* 2 (1962). https://operaismoinenglish.wordpress.com/2013/06/13/factory-and-society/. For an extension of this thesis of the social factory into the digital world, see Christian Fuchs, *Social Media: A Critical Introduction* (London: SAGE Publications, 2013), p. 118.

34. Antonio Negri, *The Politics of Subversion: A Manifesto for the Twenty-First Century* (Cambridge: Polity, 1989), p. 79.

35. Mariarosa Dalla Costa and Selma James, *The Power of Women and the Subversion of the Community* (Bristol: Falling Wall Press, 1972).

36. Selma James, *Sex, Race and Class, the Perspective of Winning: A Selection of Writings, 1952–2011* (Oakland: PM Press, 2012), p. 51.
37. Srnicek, *Platform Capitalism*.
38. Karl Marx and Friedrich Engels, *The Communist Manifesto* (London: Verso, 1998), p. 38.
39. Wendy Brown, *Undoing the Demos: Neoliberalism's Stealth Revolution* (New York: Zone Books, 2017).
40. David A. Banks, 'Subscriber City: What Happens When You Need an App to Access Anything', *Real Life*, 26 October 2020. https://reallifemag.com/subscriber-city/; Jathan Sadowski, 'How to Overcome Digital Oppression in Smart Cities', *Red Pepper*, 29 September 2017. www.redpepper.org.uk/how-to-overcome-digital-oppression-in-smart-cities/.
41. Zuboff, *The Age of Surveillance Capitalism*.
42. See Evgeny Morozov, 'Capitalism's New Clothes', *Baffler*, 4 February 2019. https://thebaffler.com/latest/capitalisms-new-clothes-morozov.
43. Zuboff, *The Age of Surveillance Capitalism*, p. 30.
44. Ibid, p. 75, emphasis in original.
45. Ibid, pp. 46–7.
46. Ibid.
47. Ibid.
48. Marx, *Capital*, p. 342.
49. Mark Neocleous, 'The Political Economy of the Dead: Marx's Vampires', *The History of Political Thought* 24, no. 4 (2003), pp. 668–84.

CHAPTER 2

1. Serge Kovaleski, 'Obama's Organizing Years, Guiding Others and Finding Himself', *New York Times*, 7 July 2008. www.nytimes.com/2008/07/07/us/politics/07community.html; Robert Slayton, 'Back of the Yards Neighborhood Council', *Encyclopedia of Chicago*. www.encyclopedia.chicagohistory.org/pages/100.html.
2. MyYouTube Channel, 'Mark Zuckerberg at the 1st Facebook Communities Summit', *YouTube*. www.youtube.com/watch?v=1hvotWxPiwo.
3. Ibid.
4. See Alexis C. Madrigal, 'The Education of Mark Zuckerberg', *The Atlantic*, 20 November 2017. www.theatlantic.com/technology/archive/2017/11/the-mark-zuckerberg-theory-of-community/546290/.
5. *Huffington Post*, 'Mark Zuckerberg 2005 Interview' (2005), *Zuckerberg Transcripts* 56. https://epublications.marquette.edu/zuckerberg_files_transcripts/56.
6. Facebook, 'Graph Search Beta Launch' (2013), *Zuckerberg Transcripts* 256. https://epublications.marquette.edu/zuckerberg_files_transcripts/256.
7. Mark Zuckerberg, 'Facebook F8 Keynote Presentation', 24 May 2007. https://about.fb.com/news/2007/05/facebook-unveils-platform-for-developers-of-social-applications/.

8. Huffington Post, 'Mark Zuckerberg 2005 Interview' (2005), *Zuckerberg Transcripts* 56. https://epublications.marquette.edu/zuckerberg_files_transcripts/56.

9. David Kirkpatrick, *The Facebook Effect: The Inside Story of the Company That Is Connecting the World* (New York: Simon & Schuster, 2010), p. 42.

10. Mark Zuckerberg, 'Building Global Community' (2017), *Zuckerberg Transcripts* 989. https://epublications.marquette.edu/zuckerberg_files_transcripts/989.

11. Mark Zuckerberg, 'First Ever Live Q&A on Facebook (with Jerry Seinfeld)' (2016), *Zuckerberg Transcripts* 263. https://epublications.marquette.edu/zuckerberg_files_transcripts/263.

12. Mark Zuckerberg, 'Harvard Commencement 2017' (2017), *Zuckerberg Videos*, Video 126. https://epublications.marquette.edu/zuckerberg_files_videos/126.

13. Ibid.

14. Mark Zuckerberg, 'Building Global Community' (2017), *Zuckerberg Transcripts* 989. https://epublications.marquette.edu/zuckerberg_files_transcripts/989.

15. Ibid.

16. Ibid.

17. Jean-Luc Nancy, *The Inoperative Community* (Minneapolis: University of Minnesota Press, 1991), p. 9, emphasis in original.

18. Robert Putnam, *Bowling Alone: The Collapse and Revival of American Community* (New York: Simon & Schuster, 2000).

19. David Harvey, *A Brief History of Neoliberalism* (Oxford: Oxford University Press, 2005).

20. Zuckerberg, 'Building Global Community'.

21. Ibid.

22. Roy Baumeister and Mark Leary, 'The Need to Belong: Desire for Interpersonal Attachments as a Fundamental Human Motivation', *Psychological Bulletin* 117, no. 3 (1995) pp. 497–529.

23. Companies MarketcCap, 'Largest Companies by Market Cap'. https://companiesmarketcap.com/facebook/marketcap/.

24. Statista, 'Facebook: Number of Monthly Active Users Worldwide 2008–2020', *Statista*.www.statista.com/statistics/264810/number-of-monthly-active-facebook-users-worldwide/.

25. Facebook IQ, 'Gen Z: Getting to Know the "Me is We" Generation', Facebook, 22 October 2019. www.facebook.com/business/news/insights/generation-z.

26. Facebook Investor Relations, 'Facebook Reports First Quarter 2021 Results', Facebook. https://investor.fb.com/investor-news/press-release-details/2021/Facebook-Reports-First-Quarter-2021-Results/default.aspx.

27. Casey Newton, 'Facebook Usage and Revenue Continue to Grow as the Pandemic Rages on', *The Verge*, 30 July 2020. www.theverge.com/2020/7/30/21348308/facebook-earnings-q2-2020-pandemic-revenue-usage-growth.

28. See Tim Hwang, *Subprime Attention Crisis: Advertising and the Time Bomb at the Heart of the Internet* (New York: FSG Originals, Logic, 2020).
29. Srnicek, *Platform Capitalism*, p. 13.
30. For an introduction to exploitation theory, see Nicholas Vrousalis, 'Exploitation: A Primer', *Philosophy Compass* 13, no. 2 (2018).
31. On the exploitation of user-generated content by technology companies, see Christian Fuchs, 'Labor in Informational Capitalism and on the Internet', *The Information Society* 26, no. 3 (2010), pp. 179–96. See also Adam Arvidsson and Elanor Colleoni, 'Value in Informational Capitalism and on the Internet', *The Information Society* 28, no. 3 (2012), pp. 135–50.
32. On Marx's theory of exploitation, see G. A. Cohen, *Karl Marx's Theory of History: A Defense* (Princeton: Princeton University Press, 1978), pp. 332–3. For a global and intersectional analysis of exploitation, see Maeve McKeown, 'Global Structural Exploitation: Towards an Intersectional Definition', *Global Justice: Theory Practice Rhetoric* 9, no. 2 (2016), pp. 155–77.
33. Tiziana Terranova, 'Free Labor: Producing Culture for the Digital Economy', *Social Text* 18, no. 2 (2000), pp. 33–58.
34. Statista, 'Leading Facebook Usage Reasons According to Users in the United States As of 3rd Quarter 2019', *Statista*, 23 September 2020. www.statista.com/statistics/972892/reasons-being-on-facebook-usa/.
35. Tithi Bhattacharya, 'Introduction: Mapping Social Reproduction Theory', in Tithi Bhattacharya (ed.), *Social Reproduction Theory: Remapping Class, Recentering Oppression* (London: Pluto Press, 2017), p. 1.
36. Vrousalis, 'Exploitation: A Primer'.
37. Karl Marx, 'Critique of the Gotha Programme'. www.marxists.org/archive/marx/works/1875/gotha/cho2.htm\.
38. Emily Stuart, 'Zuckerberg Is Essentially Untouchable at Facebook', *Vox*, 16 December 2018. www.vox.com/technology/2018/11/19/18099011/mark-zuckerberg-facebook-stock-nyt-wsj.
39. Laura Raphael, 'Mark Zuckerberg Called People Who Handed Over Their Data "Dumb F****"', *Esquire*, 23 March 2021. www.esquire.com/uk/latest-news/a19490586/mark-zuckerberg-called-people-who-handed-over-their-data-dumb-f/.
40. Marx, *Capital*, p. 885.
41. UK Parliament, 'Enclosing the Land', 2020. www.parliament.uk/about/living-heritage/transformingsociety/towncountry/landscape/overview/enclosingland/.

CHAPTER 3

1. Greylock Partners, 'Blitzscaling 18: Brian Chesky on Launching Airbnb and the Challenges of Scale', *YouTube*, 30 November 2015. www.youtube.com/watch?v=W6o8u6sBFpo.
2. Airbnb, 'Celebrating Our Community | Airbnb', *YouTube*, 7 March 2017. www.youtube.com/watch?v=zS6zVHJYopg.
3. Ibid.

4. Douglas Atkin, *The Culting of Brands: Turn Your Customers into True Believers* (New York: Portfolio, 2004).
5. CMX, 'Global Head of Community @ Airbnb – CMX Summit 2014', *YouTube*, 28 December 2014. www.youtube.com/watch?v=X-PN5WWytg0&.
6. Douglas Atkin, 'How Airbnb Found Its Purpose and Why It's a Good One', *Medium*, 10 March 2019, emphasis in original. https://medium.com/@douglas.atkin/how-airbnb-found-its-purpose-and-why-its-a-good-one-b5c987c0c216.
7. Ibid.
8. Brian Chesky, 'Belong Anywhere', *Medium*, 16 July 2014. https://medium.com/@bchesky/belong-anywhere-ccf42702d010.
9. Airbnb, 'Airbnb Introduces the Bélo: The Story of a Symbol of Belonging | Airbnb', *YouTube*, 24 July 2014. www.youtube.com/watch?v=nMITXMrrVQU.
10. CMX, 'Global Head of Community @ Airbnb – CMX Summit 2014'.
11. Ibid.
12. Airbnb Citizen, 'Organizing in 100 Cities: The Airbnb Host Movement', blog post, 5 November 2015. Quoted in Niels van Doorn, 'A New Institution on the Block: On Platform Urbanism and Airbnb Citizenship', *New Media & Society* 22, no. 10 (2020).
13. Ibid.
14. Airbnb Citizen, 'Learn More about Home Sharing Clubs', www.airbnbcitizen.com/clubs/faq.
15. Airbnb, 'Community Organiser (Fixed Term Contract)', *Velvet Jobs*. www.velvetjobs.com/job-posting/community-organiser-fixed-term-contract-399585.
16. Ibid.
17. Dan Carrier, 'Airbnb Hosts Hit Back: We Offer a Good Service!', *Islington Tribune*, 16 April 2018. http://islingtontribune.com/article/airbnb-hosts-hit-back-we-offer-a-good-service.
18. Kim-Mai Cutler, 'Airbnb Proposition F and the Shared Hypocrisy of the Bay Area', 3 November 2015. https://techcrunch.com/2015/11/03/prop-f/.
19. CMX, 'Global Head of Community @ Airbnb – CMX Summit 2014'.
20. Ibid.
21. Airbnb, 'Airbnb Policy Tool Chest'. www.airbnbcitizen.com/airbnb-policy-tool-chest/.
22. Mike Miller, 'Alinsky for the Left: The Politics of Community Organising', *Dissent* (Winter 2010). www.dissentmagazine.org/article/alinsky-for-the-left-the-politics-of-community-organizing.
23. Ibid.
24. Hahrie Han and Elizabeth McKenna, *Groundbreakers: How Obama's 2.2 Million Volunteers Transformed Campaigning in America* (Oxford: Oxford University Press, 2015).
25. Airbnb Resource Centre, 'CEO Brian Chesky on Travel Trends and Our New Host Campaign', 18 February 2021. www.airbnb.co.uk/resources/

hosting-homes/a/ceo-brian-chesky-on-travel-trends-and-our-new-host-campaign-325.

26. Recode Staff, 'Airbnb CEO Brian Chesky at Code 2018', *Vox*, 30 May 2018. www.vox.com/2018/5/30/17397156/airbnb-ceo-brian-chesky-transcript-code-2018.

27. *Transparent*, 'What the Data Says: Transparent's Take on the State of Airbnb at IPO', https://seetransparent.com/en/airbnb-ipo/who-are-todays-airbnb-hosts-and-how-loyal-are-they/#distribution-of-listings-by-owner-size-since-august-2017.

28. George Lakoff, *Don't Think of an Elephant! Know Your Values and Frame the Debate* (Vermont: Chelsea Green Publishing, 2004).

29. Airbnb Newsroom, 'An Update on Our Work to Serve All Stakeholders', 17 January 2020. https://news.airbnb.com/serving-all-stakeholders/.

30. Recode Staff, 'Airbnb CEO Brian Chesky at Code 2018', emphasis added.

31. Ibid.

32. Josh Bivens, 'The Economic Costs and Benefits of Airbnb', Economic Policy Institute, 30 January 2019. www.epi.org/files/pdf/157766.pdf.

33. Kyle Barron, Edward Kung and Davide Proserpio, 'When Airbnb Listings in a City Increase, So Do Rent Prices', *Harvard Business Review*, 17 April 2019. https://hbr.org/2019/04/research-when-airbnb-listings-in-a-city-increase-so-do-rent-prices.

34. Niko Kommenda, Helen Pidd and Libby Brooks, 'Revealed: The Areas in the UK with One Airbnb for Every Four Homes', *The Guardian*, 20 February 2020. www.theguardian.com/technology/2020/feb/20/revealed-the-areas-in-the-uk-with-one-airbnb-for-every-four-homes.

35. Olivia Carville, Andre Tartar and Jeremy C. F. Lin 'Airbnb to America's Big Cities: See You in Court', *Bloomberg*, 14 February 2020. www.bloomberg.com/graphics/2020-airbnb-ipo-challenges/.

36. Paris Martineau, 'Inside Airbnb's Guerilla War against Local Governments', *Wired*, 20 March 2019. www.wired.com/story/inside-airbnbs-guerrilla-war-against-local-governments/.

37. Nieuwsarchief, 'Cities Alarmed about European Protection of Holiday Rental', 19 June 2019. www.amsterdam.nl/bestuur-organisatie/college/wethouder/laurens-ivens/persberichten/press-release-cities-alarmed-about/.

38. Reuters Staff, 'Airbnb Backs Creation of EU Digital Regulator after Court Win', 2020. https://jp.reuters.com/article/instant-article/idUSKBN1ZS1IB.

39. CMX, 'Global Head of Community @ Airbnb – CMX Summit 2014'.

40. Carville, Tartar and Lin, 'Airbnb to America's Big Cities: See You in Court'.

41. Inside Airbnb. http://insideairbnb.com.

42. Elizabeth Pollman and Jordan M. Barry, 'Regulatory Entrepreneurship', *Southern California Law Review* 90 (2017), p. 383.

43. Ibid.

44. Airbnb Citizen. Quoted in van Doorn, 'A New Institution on the Block: On Platform Urbanism and Airbnb Citizenship'.

45. Airbnb, 'Airbnb Launches City Portal: A First-of-Its-Kind Resource for Governments', *Airbnb News*, 23 September 2020. https://news.airbnb.com/cityportal/.

46. Airbnb, 'Supporting Communities | Airbnb Citizen', *YouTube*, 6 December 2019. www.youtube.com/watch?v=uc82IRmlYR8.

47. Recode Staff, 'Airbnb CEO Brian Chesky at Code 2018'.

48. Brian Chesky, 'Our Commitment to Communities around the World', *Airbnb Blog*, 11 November 2015. https://blog.atairbnb.com/our-commitment-to-communities-around-the-world/.

49. Milton Friedman, 'A Friedman Doctrine – The Social Responsibility of Business Is to Increase Its Profits', *New York Times*, 13 September 1970. www.nytimes.com/1970/09/13/archives/a-friedman-doctrine-the-social-responsibility-of-business-is-to.html.

50. Will Hutton, *The State We're In* (London: Penguin Vintage, 2017).

51. Tony Blair, 'Tony Blair Outlines to a Singapore Business Forum His Vision of a Revitalised British Economy: A Stake in the Future', *The Herald Scotland*, 8 January 1996. www.heraldscotland.com/news/12054287.tony-blair-outlines-to-a-singapore-business-forum-his-vision-of-a-revitalised-british-economy-a-stake-in-the-future/.

52. British Labour Party 1997 Manifesto. www.labour-party.org.uk/manifestos/1997/1997-labour-manifesto.shtml.

53. Quoted in Robert Carr, *March of the Moderates: Bill Clinton, Tony Blair, and the Rebirth of Progressive Politics* (London and New York: I.B. Tauris, 2019), p. 195.

54. Business Roundtable, 'Business Roundtable Redefines the Purpose of a Corporation to Promote "An Economy that Serves All Americans"', 19 August 2019. www.businessroundtable.org/business-roundtable-redefines-the-purpose-of-a-corporation-to-promote-an-economy-that-serves-all-americans.

55. Ibid.

56. Ibid.

57. Klaus Schwab, 'Davos Manifesto 2020: The Universal Purpose of a Company in the Fourth Industrial Revolution', World Economic Forum, 2 December 2019. www.weforum.org/agenda/2019/12/davos-manifesto-2020-the-universal-purpose-of-a-company-in-the-fourth-industrial-revolution/.

58. Airbnb, 'An Update on Our Work to Serve All Stakeholders'.

59. Chris Johnston et al., 'Airbnb Value Shoots to Over $100bn in Phenomenal Wall Street Debut', *The Telegraph*, 10 December 2020. www.telegraph.co.uk/technology/2020/12/10/tech-news-live-facebook-instagram-whastapp-airbnb-ipo/.

CHAPTER 4

1. Philadelphia Police, tweet on 17 October 2018. https://twitter.com/PhillyPolice/status/1052371210384891904.

2. For a detailed analysis, see Josh Simons and Dipayan Ghosh, 'Utilities for Democracy: Why and How the Algorithmic Infrastructure of Facebook and Google Must Be Regulated', *Brookings*, August 2020. www.brookings.edu/wp-content/uploads/2020/08/FP_20200908_facebook_google_algorithm_simons_ghosh.pdf.

3. See Satoko Kishimoto and Olivier Petitjean eds, 'Reclaiming Public Services: How Cities and Citizens Are Turning Back Privatisation', *Transnational Institute*, Amsterdam and Paris, June 2017.

4. Consumer Reports, 'Platform Perceptions: Consumer Attitudes on Competition and Fairness in Online Platforms', September 2020. https://advocacy.consumerreports.org/wp-content/uploads/2020/09/FINAL-CR-survey-report.platformperceptions-consumer-attitudes-.september-2020.pdf.

5. Jedidiah Yueh, 'GDPR Will Make Big Tech Even Bigger', *Forbes*, 26 June 2018. www.forbes.com/sites/forbestechcouncil/2018/06/26/gdpr-will-make-big-tech-even-bigger/.

6. Andrew Yang, 'Make Companies Pay You for Your Data', *Los Angeles Times*, 23 June 2020. www.latimes.com/opinion/story/2020-06-23/andrew-yang-data-dividend-tech-privacy.

7. HBR Editors, 'With Big Data Comes Big Responsibility', *Harvard Business Review*, November 2014. https://hbr.org/2014/11/with-big-data-comes-big-responsibility.

8. Michelle Gao, 'Facebook Makes More Money Per User than Rivals, But It's Running Out of Growth Options', *CNBC*, 3 November 2020. www.cnbc.com/2020/11/03/facebooks-average-revenue-per-user-leads-social-media-companies.html.

9. Mark Zuckerberg, 'Yes, We Need Regulation – But We Can't Do It on Our Own', *Independent.ie*, 30 March 2019. www.independent.ie/business/technology/mark-zuckerberg-yes-we-need-regulation-but-we-cant-do-it-on-our-own-37967115.html.

10. Nicola Slawson, 'Faceblock Campaign Urges Users to Boycott Facebook for a Day', *The Guardian*, 7 April 2018. www.theguardian.com/technology/2018/apr/07/faceblock-campaign-urges-users-boycott-facebook-for-one-day-protest-cambridge-analytica-scandal.

11. Tiffany Hsu and Gillian Friedman, 'CVS, Dunkin', Lego: The Brands Pulling Ads from Facebook over Hate Speech', *New York Times*, 26 June 2020. www.nytimes.com/2020/06/26/business/media/Facebook-advertising-boycott.html.

12. Elizabeth Lopatto, 'In the Pandemic Economy, Tech Companies Are Raking It in', *The Verge*, 30 July 2020. www.theverge.com/2020/7/30/21348652/pandemic-earnings-antitrust-google-facebook-apple-amazon.

13. Brian Fung, 'The Hard Truth About the Facebook Ad Boycott: Nothing Matters But Zuckerberg', *CNN*, 26 June 2020. https://edition.cnn.com/2020/06/26/tech/facebook-boycott/index.html.

14. Dominic Rusche, 'Mark Zuckerberg: Advertisers' Boycott of Facebook Will End 'Soon Enough'', *The Guardian*, 2 July 2020. www.theguardian.

com/technology/2020/jul/02/mark-zuckerberg-advertisers-boycott-facebook-back-soon-enough.

15. Chris Hughes, 'It's Time to Break up Facebook', *New York Times*, 9 May 2019. www.nytimes.com/2019/05/09/opinion/sunday/chris-hughes-facebook-zuckerberg.html.

16. See *Standard Oil Co. of New Jersey* v. *United States*, 221 U.S. 1.

17. Makena Kelly, 'Facebook Plans to Tie Itself Together as Regulators Debate Tearing It Apart', *The Verge*, 7 March 2019. www.theverge.com/2019/3/7/18254717/facebook-instagram-whatsapp-regulation-antitrust-mark-zuckerberg-klobuchar-hawley-blumenthal.

18. Elizabeth Warren, 'How We Can Break Up Big Tech', *Warren Democrats*, 8 March 2019. https://elizabethwarren.com/plans/break-up-big-tech.

19. Adi Robertson and Russell Brandom, 'Congress Releases Blockbuster Tech Antitrust Report', *The Verge*, 6 October 2020. www.theverge.com/2020/10/6/21504814/congress-antitrust-report-house-judiciary-committee-apple-google-amazon-facebook.

20. Jerrold Natler et al., 'Investigation of Competition in Digital Markets', Majority Staff Report and Recommendations. Subcommittee on Antitrust, Commercial and Administrative Law of the Committee of the Judiciary, 2020. https://judiciary.house.gov/uploadedfiles/competition_in_digital_markets.pdf.

21. The White House, 'Fact Sheet: Executive Order on Promoting Competition in the American Economy', *The White House Briefing Room*, 9 July 2021. www.whitehouse.gov/briefing-room/statements-releases/2021/07/09/fact-sheet-executive-order-on-promoting-competition-in-the-american-economy/.

22. Gov.uk, 'Government Unveils Proposals to Increase Competition in UK Digital Economy', 20 July 2021. www.gov.uk/government/news/government-unveils-proposals-to-increase-competition-in-uk-digital-economy.

23. Simons and Ghosh, 'Utilities for Democracy'.

24. Ibid.

25. Oberlo, 'Search Engine Market Share in 2020'. www.oberlo.com/statistics/search-engine-market-share; Oberlo, 'Facebook Statistics'. www.oberlo.com/blog/facebook-statistics.

26. Simons and Ghosh, 'Utilities for Democracy'. On the history of the doctrine of public utility, see William J. Novak, 'The Public Utility Idea and the Origins of Modern Business Regulation', in Naomi R. Lamoreaux and William J. Novak (eds), *Corporations and American Democracy* (Cambridge, MA: Harvard University Press, 2017), pp. 139–76.

27. *Munn* v. *Illinois*, 94 U.S. 113 (1877). www.loc.gov/item/usrep094113/.

28. William J. Novak, 'Law and the Social Control of American Capitalism', *Emory Law Journal* 60, no. 2 (2010).

29. K. Sabeel Rahman, 'The New Utilities: Private Power, Social Infrastructure, and the Revival of the Public Utility Concept', *Cardozo Law Review* 39, no. 5 (2018), pp. 1621–89. http://cardozolawreview.com/the-newutilities-

private-power-social-infrastructure-and-the-revival-of-the-public-utility-concept/; K. Sabeel Rahman and Zephyr Teachout, 'From Private Bads to Public Goods: Adapting Public Utility Regulation for Informational Infrastructure', *The Knight First Amendment Institute*, 4 February 2020. https://knightcolumbia.org/content/from-private-bads-to-public-goods-adapting-public-utility-regulation-for-informational-infrastructure.

30. Charles Webster, *The National Health Service: A Political History* (Oxford: Oxford University Press, 1998), p. 26.

31. Sylvain Duranton et al., 'The 2017 European Railway Performance Index (RPI)', Boston Consulting Group, April 2017. www.bcg.com/publications/2017/transportation-travel-tourism-2017-european-railway-performance-index.

32. *The Highland Times*, 'Scots Water Bills Cheaper than Privatised Tory Run England', 22 February 2020. www.thehighlandtimes.com/news/2020/02/22/scots-water-bills-cheaper-than-privatised-tory-run-england/.

33. Kishimoto and Petitjean, 'Reclaiming Public Services'.

34. WeOwnIt, 'Public Ownership is Popular'. https://weownit.org.uk/public-solutions/support-public-ownership. For other contexts, see Thomas M. Hanna, 'Public Ownership in the United States and around the World', in *Our Common Wealth: The Return of Public Ownership in the United States* (Manchester: Manchester University Press, 2017).

35. Anna Coote and Andrew Percy, *The Case for Universal Basic Services* (London: Wiley, 2020).

36. Labour Party, 'Labour Party Manifesto 2019'. https://labour.org.uk/manifesto-2019.

37. Josiah Ober, 'The Original Meaning of "Democracy": Capacity to Do Things, Not Majority Rule', *Constellations* 15, no. 1 (2008), pp. 3–9.

38. See Josiah Ober, 'What the Ancient Greeks Can Tell Us about Democracy', *Annual Review of Political Science* 11 (2008), pp. 67–91.

39. Peter Marsh, *Joseph Chamberlain: Entrepreneur in Politics* (New Haven: Yale University Press, 1994).

40. Borough of Birmingham, *Short History of the Passing of the Birmingham (Corporation) Gas Act and Birmingham (Corporation) Water Act with Speeches of the Mayor (Joseph Chamberlain)* (Birmingham, 1875) 9.

41. Ibid.

42. Jules P. Gehrke, 'A Radical Endeavour: Joseph Chamberlain and the Emergence of Municipal Socialism in Birmingham', *American Journal of Economics and Sociology* 75, no. 1 (2016), pp. 23–57.

43. Sidney Webb, *English Progress towards Social Democracy* (London: The Fabian Society, 1893), p. 1.

44. Eden Medina, *Cybernetic Revolutionaries: Technology and Politics in Allende's Chile* (Cambridge, MA: MIT Press, 2014).

45. Ibid.

46. Quoted in ibid., p. 3.

47. Andrew Cumbers, *Reclaiming Public Ownership: Making Space for Economic Democracy* (London: Zed Books, 2012), pp. 33–5. See also Johan Wilner

and David Parker, 'The Performance of Public and Private Enterprise under Conditions of Active and Passive Ownership and Competition and Monopoly', *Journal of Economics* 90, no. 3 (2007).

48. Ha-Joon Chang, *State-Owned Enterprise Reform* (New York: United Nations DESA, 2007).

49. Robert Milward, 'State Enterprise in Britain in the Twentieth Century', in Pier Angelo Toninelli (ed.), *The Rise and Fall of State-Owned Enterprise in the Western World* (Cambridge: Cambridge University Press, 2000), pp. 170–3.

50. Mariana Mazzucato, *The Entrepreneurial State: Debunking Public vs. Private Sector Myths* (London: Penguin, 2018).

51. Ibid., 70.

52. Konstantin Kakaes, 'What Economists Get Wrong about Science and Technology', *Slate*, 17 May 2012. https://slate.com/technology/2012/05/robert-solow-tyler-cowen-and-other-economists-misunderstand-science-and-technology.html.

CHAPTER 5

1. On Cole's often underacknowledged influence on the British workers' movement, see Neil Riddell, '"The Age of Cole"? G. D. H. Cole and the British Labour Movement 1929–1933', *The Historical Journal* 38, no. 4 (1995), pp. 933–57.

2. For an overview of Otto Neurath's writings, see the introduction by Thomas Uebel in Robert Cohen and Thomas Uebel eds, *Otto Neurath: Economic Writings. Selections 1904–1945* (New York: Kluwer Publishers, 2004), pp. 1–108.

3. Quentin Skinner, *Liberty before Liberalism* (Cambridge: Cambridge University Press, 1996), p. 117.

4. G. D. H. Cole, *Guild Socialism Restated* (London: Routledge, 2011 [1920]), p. 12.

5. Ibid., p. 14.

6. Ibid., p. 6, p. 11.

7. Ibid., p. 31.

8. Mark Bevir, 'A History of Modern Pluralism', in Mark Bevir (ed.), *Modern Pluralism: Anglo-American Debates since 1880* (Cambridge: Cambridge University Press, 2012), pp. 1–20.

9. Cole, *Guild Socialism Restated*, p. 47.

10. Hanna, *Our Common Wealth*, p. 132.

11. Nicholas Vrousalis has described this as 'the socialisation dilemma'. Nicholas Vrousalis, 'Council Democracy and the Socialisation Dilemma', in James Muldoon (ed.), *Council Democracy: Towards a Democratic Socialist Politics* (London: Routledge, 2018), pp. 89–107.

12. Karl Kautsky, *The Labour Revolution* (London: Routledge, 2013), p. 204.

13. Andrew Cumbers, *The Case for Economic Democracy* (Cambridge: Polity, 2020), p. 28.

14. Simon Borkin, 'Platform Co-operatives – Solving the Capital Conundrum', *Nesta*, February 2019. https://media.nesta.org.uk/documents/Nesta_Platform_Report_FINAL-WEB_b1qZGj7.pdf.
15. Anthony W. Wright, 'Guild Socialism Revisited', *Journal of Contemporary History* 9, no. 1 (1974), p. 173.
16. Cole, *Guild Socialism Restated*, p. 32.
17. Ibid., p. 156.
18. Henry Pachter, *Socialism in History: Political Essays* (Columbia: Columbia University Press, 1984), p. 46.
19. Marx, *Capital*, p. 442.
20. On the German Revolution, see Gaard Kets and James Muldoon eds, *The German Revolution and Political Theory* (London: Palgrave Macmillan, 2019).
21. Otto Neurath, 'Der Guildensozialismus und unsere Zukunft', *Arbeiter-Zeitung* 48, 18 February 1921.
22. Neurath, 'Economic Plan and Calculation in Kind', in *Economic Writings*, p. 415.
23. UN Intergovernmental Panel on Climate Change (IPCC), October 2018 report.
24. Kyle Lewis and Will Stronge, *Overtime: Why We Need a Shorter Working Week* (London: Verso, 2021).
25. Neurath, 'Economic Plan and Calculation in Kind', in *Economic Writings*, p. 425.
26. Karl Kautsky, *Die Proletarische Revolution und Ihr Programm* (Berlin and Stuttgart : J. H. W. Dietz Verlag, 1922), p. 260.
27. Otto Neurath, 'Physicalism, Planning and the Social Sciences: Bricks Prepared for a Discussion v. Hayek', 26 July 1945, *The Otto Neurath Nachlass in Haarlem* 202 K.56. Quoted in John O'Neil, 'Pluralism and Economic Institutions', *Otto Neurath's Economics in Context*, pp. 77–100.
28. Neurath, 'Economic Plan and Calculation in Kind', in *Economic Writings*, p. 447.
29. Neurath, 'A System of Socialisation', in *Economic Writings*, p. 356.
30. Max Weber, *Economy and Society: An Outline of Interpretive Sociology*, eds Guenther Roth and Claus Wittich (Berkeley: University of California Press, 1978), p. 101.
31. Benjamin Braun, 'Asset Manager Capitalism as a Corporate Governance Regime', in J. S. Hacker, A. Hertel-Fernandez, P. Pierson and K. Thelen (eds), *American Political Economy: Politics, Markets, and Power* (New York: Cambridge University Press, forthcoming).
32. Peter Drucker, *The Unseen Revolution: How Pension Fund Socialism Came to America* (Oxford: Butterworth-Heinemann, 1976).
33. Mathew Lawrence and Loren King, 'Examining the Inclusive Ownership Fund', *Common Wealth*, 13 November 2019. www.common-wealth.co.uk/reports/examining-the-inclusive-ownership-fund.
34. David McLaughlin and Annie Massa, 'The Hidden Dangers of the Great Index Fund Takeover', *Bloomberg*, 9 January 2020. www.bloomberg.

com/news/features/2020-01-09/the-hidden-dangers-of-the-great-index-fund-takeover.

35. Neurath, 'Total Socialisation', in *Economic Writings*, p. 390.

36. Ibid., p. 401.

37. For one possible model of such a system see Pat Devine, *Democracy and Economic Planning: The Political Economy of a Self-governing Society* (London: Routledge, 1988).

38. See for example Joseph Stiglitz, *Wither Socialism* (Cambridge, MA: MIT Press, 1994), p. 9.

39. This includes Fred M. Taylor and Oskar R. Lange, *On the Economic Theory of Socialism* (Minneapolis: University of Minnesota Press, 1938); Alec Nove, *The Economics of Feasible Socialism* (London: Routledge, 1983); John Roemer, *A Future for Socialism* (Cambridge, MA: Harvard University Press, 1994); David Schweickart, *After Capitalism* (London: Rowman & Littlefield 2011).

40. Friedrich Hayek, *The Road to Serfdom* (Chicago: The University of Chicago Press, 1944), 149.

41. See Friedrich Hayek, 'The Use of Knowledge in Society', in *Individualism and Economic Order* (Chicago: University of Chicago Press, 1948), pp. 77–91.

42. Pat Devine, 'Participatory Planning through Negotiated Coordination', *Science & Society* 66, no. 1 (2002), p. 75.

43. Evgeny Morozov, 'Digital Socialism? The Calculation Debate in the Age of Big Data', *New Left Review* 116/117 (2019).

44. David Miller, 'Social Democracy', in Edward Craig (ed.), *The Routledge Encyclopedia of Philosophy* (London: Routledge, 1998), p. 8.

45. G. D. H. Cole, 'For Democracy', in *Towards a Libertarian Socialism* (Chico: AK Press, 2021).

46. Neurath, 'Total Socialisation', in *Economic Writings*, p. 402.

47. Ibid.

48. Cole, *Guild Socialism Restated*, p. 7.

CHAPTER 6

1. On platform co-operatives, see Trebor Scholz, 'Platform Cooperativism: Challenging the Corporate Sharing Economy', Rosa Luxemburg Stiftung, New York City, 2016; Trebor Scholz and Nathan Schneider eds, *Ours to Hack and Own: The Rise of Platform Cooperativism, a New Vision for the Future of Work and a Fairer Internet* (New York: OR Books, 2016).

2. Platform Cooperativism Consortium. https://platform.coop/.

3. Bertie Russell, 'Beyond the Local Trap: New Municipalism and the Rise of the Fearless Cities', *Antipode: A Radical Journal of Geography* (2019). Laura Roth, 'Which Municipalism? Let's Be Choosy', *openDemocracy*, 2 January 2019. www.opendemocracy.net/en/can-europe-make-it/which-municipalism-lets-be-choosy/. See also www.fearlesscities.com.

4. UP&GO. www.upandgo.coop/.

5. Trebor Scholz, *Uberworked and Underpaid: How Workers Are Disrupting the Digital Economy* (London: Polity, 2016), pp. 184–92.
6. Marisol Sandoval, 'Entrepreneurial Activism? Platform Cooperativism between Subversion and Co-optation', *Critical Sociology* 34, no. 1 (2019), pp. 51–79.
7. Ed Mayo ed., 'The Co-operative Advantage: Innovation, Co-operation and Why Sharing Business Ownership Is Good for Britain', Co-operatives UK, London, 2015.
8. Deborah Linton, 'David Cameron: Co-op Is Victim of Poor Leadership', *Manchester Evening News*, 3 April 2014. www.manchestereveningnews.co.uk/news/greater-manchester-news/david-cameron-cheadle-stockport-co-op-6910749.
9. Karl Marx, *Inaugural Address and Provisional Rules of the International Working Men's Association*. www.marxists.org/archive/marx/works/1864/10/27.htm.
10. Rosa Luxemburg, *Social Reform or Revolution*. www.marxists.org/archive/luxemburg/1900/reform-revolution/.
11. Maurits de Jongh, 'Public Goods and the Commons: Opposites or Complements?' *Political Theory* (2020) https://doi.org/10.1177/0090591720979916.
12. Barcelona International Welcome, 'First Projects at the Coòpolis Incubator for Cooperatives'. www.barcelona.cat/internationalwelcome/en/noticia/first-projects-at-the-coopolis-incubator-for-cooperatives_992619.
13. Leandro Minuchin et al., 'Municipal Logistics: Popular Infrastructures and Southern Urbanisms during the Pandemic', *Minim*, December 2020. https://minim-municipalism.org/reports/report-4-municipal-logistics-popular-infrastructures-and-southern-urbanisms-during-the-pandemic.
14. Lucas Cumisky, 'Tech Co-ops Circulating Cash in Finsbury Park to Combat Offshore "Wealth Extraction"', *Islington Gazette*, 17 July 2019. www.islingtongazette.co.uk/news/outlandish-trains-tech-co-ops-to-keep-cash-circulating-in-3820974.
15. www.wings.coop.
16. Keir Milburn and Bertie Russell, 'Public–Common Partnerships: Building New Circuits of Collective Ownership', *Common Wealth*, 27 June 2019. www.common-wealth.co.uk/reports/public-common-partnerships-building-new-circuits-of-collective-ownership.
17. Ibid.
18. Niels van Doorn, 'Platform Labor: On the Gendered and Racialized Exploitation of Low-Income Service Work in the "On-demand" Economy', *Information, Communication & Society* 20, no. 6 (2017), pp. 898–914.
19. Quoted in Scholz, *Uberworked and Underpaid*, p. 173.
20. Alan Wiig, 'The Empty Rhetoric of the Smart City: From Digital Inclusion to Economic Promotion in Philadelphia', *Urban Geography* 37, no. 4 (2016).
21. Jathan Sadowski, 'The Captured City', *Real Life Magazine*, 12 November 2019. https://reallifemag.com/the-captured-city/. See also Jathan Sadowski, *Too Smart: How Digital Capitalism Is Extracting Data, Controlling Our Lives, and Taking over the World* (Cambridge, MA: MIT Press, 2020), pp. 129–60.

22. Sommer Mathis and Alexandra Kanik, 'Why You'll Be Hearing a Lot Less about "Smart Cities"', *City Monitor*, 18 February 2021. https://citymonitor. ai/government/why-youll-be-hearing-a-lot-less-about-smart-cities.

23. Andrew J. Hawkins, 'Alphabet's Sidewalk Labs Shuts Down Toronto Smart City Project', *The Verge*, 7 May 2020. www.theverge.com/2020/5/7/21250594/ alphabet-sidewalk-labs-toronto-quayside-shutting-down.

24. Barcelona: Urban Platform. www.c40.org/profiles/2014-barcelona.

25. Decidim. https://decidim.org/.

26. DECODE project. https://decodeproject.eu/.

27. Of particular note are the new theoretical models of citizen-led data governance that are growing out of the experiments. See Theo Bass and Rosalyn Old, 'Common Knowledge: Citizen-Led Data Governance for Better Cities', *Nesta*, January 2020. https://media.nesta.org.uk/documents/ DECODE_Common_Knowledge_Citizen_led_data_governance_for_ better_cities_Jan_2020.pdf.

28. James Muldoon, 'Airbnb Has Been Rocked by COVID-19: Do We Really Want to See It Recover?' *openDemocracy*, 4 April 2020. www. opendemocracy.net/en/oureconomy/airbnb-has-been-rocked-covid-19-should-it-be-allowed-recover/.

29. See, for example, Uber allowing prominent scholars to publish articles based on proprietary data and non-replicable analysis that were used as part of the company's PR campaigns. Hubert Horan, 'Uber's "Academic Research" Program: How to Use Famous Economists to Spread Corporate Narratives', *ProMarket*, 5 December 2019. https://promarket.org/2019/12/05/ubers-academic-research-program-how-to-use-famous-economists-to-spread-corporate-narratives/.

30. For an examination of these issues, see Theo Bass and Rosalyn Old, 'Common Knowledge: Citizen-Led Data Governance for Better Cities'.

31. Kantar, 'Public Attitudes to Science 2019', *BEIS Research Paper Number 2020/012* (2019). https://assets.publishing.service.gov.uk/government/ uploads/system/uploads/attachment_data/file/905466/public-attitudes-to-science-2019.pdf.

32. Nesta, a UK innovation foundation, has produced a typology for different forms of governance that could enhance the public value of data in addition to protecting individual privacy. See www.nesta.org.uk/blog/ new-ecosystem-trust/.

33. Ruha Benjamin, *Race after Technology: Abolitionist Tools for the New Jim Code* (New York: Polity, 2019).

34. Chainspace, 'DECODE: Powering Civic Good with a Blockchain', *Medium*, 3 December 2018. https://medium.com/chainspace/decode-powering-civic-good-with-a-blockchain-3fdf668a1826.

35. Ajuntament de Barcelona, 'Barcelona Digital City: Putting Technology at the Service of People', 2019. https://ajuntament.barcelona.cat/digital/sites/ default/files/pla_barcelona_digital_city_in.pdf.

36. ViaVan, 'Viavan Partners with Transport for London and Go-Ahead to Launch Gosutton', 28 May 2019. https://ridewithvia.com/news/viavan-partners-with-transport-for-london-and-go-ahead-to-launch-gosutton/.

37. Transport for London Budget 2020/1. http://content.tfl.gov.uk/tfl-budget-2020–21.pdf.

38. Nico Muzi, 'Uber Adds to Pollution and Traffic in European Cities Too', *Transport & Environment*, 21 November 2019. www.transportenvironment. org/press/uber-adds-pollution-and-traffic-european-cities-too.

39. TfL Dial-a-Ride. https://tfl.gov.uk/modes/dial-a-ride/.

40. New Economics Foundation, 'New Poll: 82% of Uber Users Ready to Quit the Service', *New Economics Foundation*, 29 January 2018. https:// neweconomics.org/2018/01/new-poll-82-uber-users-ready-quit-service.

41. TaxiApp. www.taxiapp.uk.com.

42. Alex Hern, 'Uber and Lyft Pull Out of Austin after Locals Vote Against Self-regulation', *The Guardian*, 9 May 2016. www.theguardian.com/ technology/2016/may/09/uber-lyft-austin-vote-against-self-regulation.

43. Jack Flagler, 'RideAustin Shuts Down Operations', *Community Impact*, 12 June 2020. https://communityimpact.com/austin/central-austin/impacts/ 2020/06/12/rideaustin-shuts-down-operations/.

44. Matthew Zeitlin, 'How Austin's Failed Attempt to Regulate Uber and Lyft Foreshadowed Today's Ride-Hailing Controversies', *Vox*, 13 September 2019. www.vox.com/the-highlight/2019/9/6/20851575/uber-lyft-drivers-austin-regulation-rideshare.

45. Nathan Schneider, '5 Ways to Take Back Tech', *The Nation*, 27 May 2015. www.thenation.com/article/archive/5-ways-take-back-tech/.

46. Douglas Murphy, 'Real Utopias: Switzerland's Housing Co-ops', *Tribune*, 18 June 2019. https://tribunemag.co.uk/2019/01/switzerland-housing-coop-cooperative.

47. Paris Marx, 'To Fix the Looming Supply Chain Crisis, Nationalize Amazon', *In These Times*, 22 March 2020. https://inthesetimes.com/article/ supply-chain-crisis-nationalize-amazon-coronavirus-covid-19.

48. Cecilia Rikap, 'What Would a State-Owned Amazon Look Like? Ask Argentina', *openDemocracy*, 24 November 2020. www.opendemocracy.net/en/ oureconomy/what-would-state-owned-amazon-look-ask-argentina/.

49. Ibid.

50. Felix Richter, 'Amazon Leads $150-Billion Cloud Market', *Statista*, 15 July 2021. www.statista.com/chart/18819/worldwide-market-share-of-leading-cloud-infrastructure-service-providers/.

51. Steven J. Vaughan-Nichols, 'Put the Internet Back under Your Control with the Freedombox', *ZDNet*, 28 April 2019. www.zdnet.com/article/ put-the-internet-back-under-your-control-with-the-freedombox/.

52. https://e-estonia.com/.

53. Ian Traynor, 'Russia Accused of Unleashing Cyberwar to Disable Estonia', *The Guardian*, 17 May 2007. www.theguardian.com/world/2007/may/17/ topstories3.russia.

54. https://e-estonia.com/solutions/e-governance/government-cloud/.

55. https://e-estonia.com/estonia-to-open-the-worlds-first-data-embassy-in-luxembourg/.

56. https://nextcloud.com/.

CHAPTER 7

1. United States National Security Commission on Artificial Intelligence, 'Final Report', March 2021. www.nscai.gov/wp-content/uploads/2021/03/Full-Report-Digital-1.pdf.

2. Michael Kwet, 'Digital Colonialism: The Evolution of US Empire', *TNI Longreads*, 4 March 2021. https://longreads.tni.org/digital-colonialism-the-evolution-of-us-empire.

3. 'Project Loon' was started by Google and still operates in some countries to test the capacity of using large balloons to spread digital connectivity. https://loon.com/.

4. Renata Avila, 'Against Digital Colonialism', in James Muldoon and Will Stronge (eds), *Platforming Equality: Policy Challenges for the Digital Economy* (London: Autonomy, 2020).

5. ITU, 'Measuring Digital Development Facts and Figures 2019', www.itu.int/en/ITU-D/Statistics/Documents/facts/FactsFigures2019.pdf.

6. For an early influential study, see Lucas D. Introna and Helen Nissenbaum, 'Shaping the Web: Why the Politics of Search Engines Matters', *The Information Society* 16 (2000), pp. 169–85.

7. Batya Friedman and David G. Hendry, *Value Sensitive Design: Shaping Technology with Moral Imagination* (Cambridge, MA: MIT Press, 2019).

8. Jack Dorsey, Twitter, 14 January 2021. https://twitter.com/jack/status/1349510769268850690.

9. Julio López, 'How to Hunt Down a Hate Group on the Internet', *Buenos Aires Times*, 6 January 2021. www.batimes.com.ar/news/opinion-and-analysis/how-to-hunt-down-a-hate-group-on-the-internet.phtml.

10. Jürgen Habermas, *The Structural Transformation of the Public Sphere: An Inquiry into a Category of Bourgeois Society*, trans. Thomas Burger (Cambridge, MA: MIT Press, 1989).

11. Tom Batchelor, 'Corbyn Says Labour Would Consider State-Owned Facebook Rival', *The Independent*, 23 August 2018. www.independent.co.uk/news/uk/politics/jeremy-corbyn-facebook-state-owned-social-media-bbc-iplayer-privacy-labour-public-ownership-a8504151.html.

12. Jordan Guiao, 'Tech-Xit: Can Australia Survive without Google and Facebook?' Centre for Responsible Technology, October 2020. https://d3n8a8pro7vhmx.cloudfront.net/theausinstitute/pages/3386/attachments/original/1603049830/P986_Techxit_Issues_Paper_2.1__Web_.pdf.

13. For an analysis, see Derek Hrynyshyn, 'Imagining Platform Socialism', *Socialist Register* 57 (2021).

14. Howard Rheingold, *The Virtual Community: Homesteading on the Electronic Frontier* (New York: Harper Perennial, 1993).

15. For a history of the WELL see Katie Hafner, *The WELL: A Story of Love, Death and Real Life in the Seminal Online Community* (New York: Carroll & Graf, 2001).

16. Rheingold, *The Virtual Community*, xix.

17. For an analysis of different systems, see Chelsea Barabas, Neha Narula and Ethan Zuckerman, 'Defending Internet Freedom through Decentralization: Back to the Future?', The Center for Civic Media & The Digital Currency Initiative MIT Media Lab, August 2017.

18. Mike Masnick, 'Protocols, Not Platforms: A Technological Approach to Free Speech', 21 August 2019. https://knightcolumbia.org/content/protocols-not-platforms-a-technological-approach-to-free-speech.

19. https://en.wikipedia.org/wiki/Mastodon_(software).

20. Barabas, Narula and Zuckerman, 'Defending Internet Freedom through Decentralization: Back to the Future?', p. 39.

21. www.eff.org/deeplinks/2019/10/adversarial-interoperability.

CHAPTER 8

1. J. S. Tan and Nataliya Nedzhvetskaya, '2020: A Year of Resistance in Tech', *Collective Action in Tech*, 31 December 2020. https://collectiveaction.tech/2020/2020-a-year-of-resistance-in-tech/.

2. Ben Tarnoff, 'The Making of the Tech Worker Movement', *Logic*, 4 May 2020. https://logicmag.io/the-making-of-the-tech-worker-movement/full-text/; Annie Palmer, 'How Amazon Keeps a Close Eye on Employee Activism to Head off Unions', *CNBC*, 24 October 2020. www.cnbc.com/2020/10/24/how-amazon-prevents-unions-by-surveilling-employee-activism.html; Noam Scheiber and Daisuke Wakabayashi, 'Google Hires Firm Known for Anti-union Efforts', *The New York Times*, 20 November 2019. www.nytimes.com/2019/11/20/technology/Google-union-consultant.html.

3. Natasha Dow Schüll, 'The Folly of Technological Solutionism: An Interview with Evgeny Morozov', *Public Books*, 9 September 2013. www.publicbooks.org/the-folly-of-technological-solutionism-an-interview-with-evgeny-morozov/.

4. Lilly Irani and Rumman Chowdhury, 'To Really "Disrupt", Tech Needs to Listen to Actual Researchers', *Wired*, 26 June 2019. www.wired.com/story/tech-needs-to-listen-to-actual-researchers/.

5. Our Data Bodies. www.odbproject.org/.

6. Tarnoff, 'The Making of the Tech Worker Movement'.

7. Kurt Vandaele, 'Collective Resistance and Organizational Creativity Amongst Europe's Platform Workers: A New Power in the Labour Movement?', in Julietta Haidar and Maarten Keune (eds), *Work and Labour Relations in Global Platform Capitalism* (Cheltenham and Geneva: Edward Elgar and ILO, 2021); Jamie Woodcock, *The Fight against Platform Capitalism: An Inquiry into the Global Struggles of the Gig Economy* (London: University of Westminster Press, 2021).

8. Callum Cant, *Riding for Deliveroo: Resistance in the New Economy* (London: Polity, 2019).
9. Michael David Maffie, 'The Role of Digital Communities in Organising Gig Workers', *Industrial Relations* 59, no. 1 (2020), pp. 123–49.
10. Tomasz Frymorgen, 'The Rise of the Unorganizable', *Jacobin*, 7 September 2016. www.jacobinmag.com/2016/09/the-rise-of-the-unorganizable/.
11. Vandaele, 'Collective Resistance and Organizational Creativity amongst Europe's Platform Workers'.
12. International Alliance of App-Based Transport Workers. https://iaatw.org/.
13. Asger Havstein Eriksen, 'Groundbreaking Agreement: Danes Can Now Order Takeaways with a Clean Conscience', *Fagblatet3F*, 27 January 2021. https://fagbladet3f.dk/node/54171.
14. Niels van Doorn, 'On the Conditions of Possibility for Worker Organizing in Platform-Based Gig Economies', *Notes from Below*, 8 June 2019. https://notesfrombelow.org/article/conditions-possibility-worker-organizing-platform.
15. Julia Ticona and Alexandra Mateescu, 'Trusted Strangers: Carework Platforms' Cultural Entrepreneurship in the On-demand Economy', *New Media & Society* 20, no. 11 (2018).
16. Niels van Doorn, Fabian Ferrari and Mark Graham, 'Migration and Migrant Labour in the Gig Economy: An Intervention'. https://ssrn.com/abstract=3622589; Dalia Gebrial, 'Dangerous Brown Workers: How Race and Migration Politics Shape the Platform Labour Market', in James Muldoon and Will Stronge (eds), *Platforming Equality: Policy Challenges for the Platform Economy* (London: Autonomy, 2020).
17. Faircrowdwork, 'Platform Reviews' (2019). http://faircrowd.work/platform-reviews/.
18. FairTube, 'FairTube E. V. Launched and Important Video', 3 February 2021. https://fairtube.info/blog/fairtube-e-v-launch-and-important-video/.
19. Steven Greenhouse, '"We Deserve More": An Amazon Warehouse's High-Stakes Union Drive', *The Guardian*, 23 February 2021. www.theguardian.com/technology/2021/feb/23/amazon-bessemer-alabama-union.
20. Clarissa Redwine, 'The ABC's of Google's New Union', *Collective Action in Tech*, 4 January 2021. https://collectiveaction.tech/2021/the-abcs-of-googles-new-union/.
21. Tech Workers Coalition. https://techworkerscoalition.org/.
22. Mark Graham, 'Regulate, Replicate, and Resist: The Conjunctural Geographies of Platform Urbanism', *Urban Geography* 41, no. 3 (2020).
23. Niels van Doorn, 'At What price? Labour Politics and Calculative Power Struggles in On-demand Food Delivery', *Work Organisation, Labour & Globalisation* 14, no. 1 (2020), pp. 136–49.
24. Phil Jones, 'Rethinking Microwork: The Invisible Labour of the Platform Economy', in *Platforming Equality*.
25. David Montgomery, *Workers' Control in America* (Cambridge: Cambridge University Press, 1979), p. 13.

26. Alexia Fernández Campbell, 'The Problem with Amazon's Speedy Shipping, in One Graphic', *Vox*, 18 October 2019. www.vox.com/identities/ 2019/10/18/20920717/amazon-shipping-workers-injuries.

27. Zephyr Teachout, *Break 'Em Up: Recovering Our Freedom from Big Ag, Big Tech, and Big Money* (New York: All Points Books, 2020).

28. Samuel Stolton, 'Dutch Deputy Prime Minister Calls for Digital Services Act Regulation against AirBnB', *Euractiv*, 9 November 2020. www.euractiv. com/section/digital/news/dutch-deputy-prime-minister-calls-for-digital-services-act-regulation-against-airbnb/.

29. Justin Nogarede, 'Governing Online Gatekeepers – Taking Power Seriously', *Foundation for European Progressive Studies*, 15 January 2021. www.feps-europe.eu/attachments/publications/governi7ng%20online%20gatekeepers %201.pdf.

30. Kenneth Haar, 'Unfairbnb: How Online Rental Platforms Use the EU to Defeat Cities' Affordable Housing Measures', Corporate Europe Observatory, May 2018. https://corporateeurope.org/sites/default/files/unfairbnb. pdf.

31. Eric Olin Wright, *Envisioning Real Utopias* (London: Verso, 2010), p. 332.

Index